THE BIBLE: FACT OR FANTASY?

Miracles, people rising from the dead, a man who claimed to be God — the Bible contains some sensational material. If these things really happened, they are vitally important for all time.

But is the Bible 'true'? Has its truth been disproved by discoveries in history, archaeology or science? Do the Bible's stories and its teaching still ring true today?

JOHN DRANE, Lecturer in Religious Studies at Stirling University, Scotland, has written popular introductions to the Old and New Testaments, and the best-selling *Jesus and the Four Gospels*. He has presented religious programmes on television. His doctoral research was on the Gnostics. In this book he brings his talents as a scholar and communicator to bear on the central question of the Bible's trustworthiness and relevance today.

THE BIBLE

Fact or Fantasy?

John Drane

A LION PAPERBACK

Oxford · Batavia · Sydney

Copyright © 1989 John Drane
This edition © 1989 Lion Publishing plc

Published by
Lion Publishing plc
Sandy Lane West, Oxford, England
ISBN 0 7459 1300 8
Lion Publishing Corporation
1705 Hubbard Avenue, Batavia, Illinois 60510, USA
ISBN 0 7459 1300 8
Albatross Books Pty Ltd
PO Box 320, Sutherland, NSW 2232, Australia
ISBN 0 7324 0138 0

Reprinted 1990

Printed and bound in Great Britain
by Cox & Wyman Ltd, Reading

Contents

1

Searching for Meaning

Dumbfounded! That was how I felt as I drove back home through the cold air of a December night. The road skirting the edge of the Scottish Highlands was not the sort on which you can drive very fast at any time. In mid-winter, there was a good chance of ice — and perhaps even a hungry stag looking for supper on the grassy verge. So I had plenty of time to think, even though the journey was little more than twenty miles.

I had been to a party! The sort of party that you're not sure it's worth going to — until it's over. It was a pretty quiet affair. Six or seven couples, some married, some living together unmarried, and one or two singles. Most of us had never met before, so we had some introductions to make. In typical Western fashion we all began to describe ourselves by reference to our work. We were a very mixed bunch, with wide-ranging expertise. An electrician, a surgeon, a forester, a bureaucrat, an engineer — and more besides. Then there was me.

'And what do you do, John?'

'Oh, I work in a university,' I replied, deliberately trying to be as vague as possible. One or two looked as if they might already have been turned off by the prospect of spending an evening with some ivory-tower academic whose knowledge was probably limited to all the things that nobody else had ever wanted to know about. But others were curious. Was I perhaps a wizard with computers? Or some kind of scientist or technologist pushing forward the frontiers of human knowledge? So the inevitable supplementary soon followed: 'And which department do you work in?'

Now I knew from experience that this could be tricky, so I opted for a fairly general reply: 'Religious Studies.' That alone can usually be guaranteed to create a slight hiatus in the conversation — and so it did. But having got this far, why turn back? Especially if you're curious to know whatever could possibly attract an apparently normal person to spend their life thinking about such a subject. In any case, it needn't all be boring: perhaps I was an expert in Islam, or Zen, or some other esoteric subject that would be good for at least a couple of minutes' worth of polite conversation. And, who knows, it might even be interesting. So someone piped up, 'Religious Studies? I suppose that will be comparative religion, then?'

By now, I had a reasonably clear idea what would happen next. For the true answer to that question can go down like a lead balloon in some circles: 'Well no. Actually I'm interested in Christian studies — I mostly teach the Bible.' Sure enough, there was an audible gasp from someone, followed by a general horrified silence. People in Britain today sometimes find talk about the Bible a bit threatening, especially in a group of people they hardly know.

For what seemed like an eternity — but cannot have been longer than about five seconds — no one spoke. The floor and the ceiling suddenly became subjects of compelling fascination! But not for long. For what I had said about myself was like letting the cork out of a well-shaken bottle of champagne. Soon, everyone was talking — to each other, but especially to me. This time I was in the hot seat! 'Do you really believe there is a God?' Followed by, 'How can a book as ancient as the Bible still make sense today?'

And what about reincarnation, or life after death? By now more than an hour had passed. One or two others had arrived to join the party — but still the subject was religion. An experienced professional counsellor began relating the case of a delinquent youth who seemed to be, as he put it, 'just a body', with no awareness of the fact that he had committed offences, nor of their consequence. As we all listened spellbound to this hair-raising tale, the person telling it confided that at the time he had wondered if this boy could have been 'possessed'. Did I think this was possible? So it went on, long into the evening. And even when the group split up into smaller circles, those who attached themselves to me still wanted to talk about religion.

Interest in the supernatural

As far as I know, my partner and I were the only practising Christians in that group. But it was obvious that virtually everyone there believed in God. Or if they didn't, they weren't sufficiently certain to say so. Moreover, even though they were all educated and intelligent people, the presence and power of the supernatural (both good and evil) was part of their world-view. And despite the fact that none of them could see much relevance in the church as they knew and experienced it, they all had an obvious fascination for the Bible, and its central figure, Jesus Christ.

Ten years ago, that would never have happened. Certainly not in Scotland. But that Christmas party is typical of situations I am finding myself in every day. Whatever the prophets of the modern media would like us to think, the fact is that allegedly 'secular' Western people are today far more religious than for many generations. The evidence is not just conversations that take place at parties: it is all around us. And you might be surprised to reflect on the sort of religion we seem to find most believable.

Twenty years ago, the film industry had every appearance of being in terminal decline. Yet today one box office success follows another. And what are these blockbusters all about? Religion, mostly. We flock in our thousands to watch fantasy films whose storylines are dominated by ideas that our grandparents would have regarded as incredible. Trance channelling, healing with crystals, reincarnation, out of the body experiences, past life recall, altered states of consciousness, UFO abductions — they are all everyday occurrences in the celluloid scenes that influence the thinking of today's world. In *Star Wars*, the hero Luke Skywalker is initiated into a league of Jedi knights by mastering 'the Force' that animates the cosmos. When the film was first screened, thousands of people greeted their friends with the words, 'May the Force be with you.' Indiana Jones first shot to fame with *Raiders of the Lost Ark*, a mystical tale based on the spiritual enigmas surrounding the biblical 'ark of the covenant'. *Indiana Jones and the Temple of Doom* shows the same hero battling for possession of a primeval magic talisman called a 'shankara stone'.

We have come to accept the possibility of intruders from other worlds. Sometimes they are friendly, like Superman or ET. More often they are menacing and pose a threat to life as we know it — as in, *The Exorcist*, or *2001*. Occasionally, they seem cuddly and amiable to start with but soon develop a sinister twist. In *Gremlins*, an innocent child's pet that looks like a cross between a hamster and a teddy bear ominously multiplies into an army of monsters whose warped sense of humour is exclusively devoted to spreading disorder and death through a small-time American town. Even the familiar and friendly Disney characters of children's cartoons have been replaced by more awesome beasts who deal in cosmic forces and spiritual power.

Take a look at some of the most popular books of our day, and you find exactly the same. Any one-horse town with a small bookstore is certain to have Scott Peck's book, *The Road Less Travelled*. It probably also stocks the writings of Hollywood star Shirley MacLaine, and Marilyn Ferguson — two women who between them have popularized a hybrid form of pop philosophy that mixes science fiction with sociology, religion, medicine, healthy living and sport. There are even books claiming to be written by disembodied beings from some other state of consciousness, channelled through human contacts. One of them, *A Course in Miracles*, is a bestseller. A 'revelation' from 'Jesus', among others, it was channelled through Helen Schucman of the psychiatry department at Columbia University, New York, in the mid-seventies. Today its three volumes have been translated into a dozen languages, and they are avidly studied in small groups throughout the world, by serious people searching for the key to life's ultimate meaning.

Television viewers in Britain have become accustomed to seeing violent struggles between police and the many thousands of religious devotees who crowd into the ancient site of Stonehenge each year at the summer solstice, hoping to make some kind of contact with the earth spirit. In America a hundred years ago, pioneers of the Wild West were baffled by the religion of the native Indians, which also focused on the 'Great Spirit'. It was, they concluded, primitive and unsophisticated. Now their great-grandchildren are reconstructing medicine wheels — circles of stones, each representing a part of the universe — at sacred sites all over the country. The Moray Firth in the north of Scotland is home to the Findhorn community, a group of people with worldwide connections who believe that this isolated spot has cosmic significance for the future of the earth, because many lines of spiritual power allegedly converge there.

All over the world, those claiming to have messages channelled from some other state of consciousness attract a great following. In Los Angeles, Gerry Bowman channels 'John the Apostle' every Sunday at midnight on radio station KIEV. In Sao Paulo, Brazil, Luiz Antonio Gasparetto hosts a weekly TV show in which he channels 'old master' artists to produce fresh paintings through his hands. Others do a similar thing in large-scale revival meetings across the United States. J.Z. Knight of Washington State is one of the best known. A former home-maker, she channels Ramtha, a 35,000-year-old warrior from the ancient world — otherwise known as 'the Ram'.

Nor is this a minority interest restricted to cranks and crackpots. Many Hollywood celebrities are sold on it as the panacea to life's problems. In 1987, Sharon Gless won an Emmy award for her part in the TV series 'Cagney and Lacey'. In her acceptance speech she claimed that her success was due to 'Lazaris', another disembodied personality — this time channelled by a retired Florida insurance consultant called Jack Pursel. In 1988, former White House chief of staff Donald T. Regan claimed that President Reagan and his wife used an astrologer to plan their lives. According to a report from Associated Press dated 3 May 1988, it was on such advice that the president insisted on signing his nuclear disarmament treaty with the Soviet leader Mikhail Gorbachev at exactly 1.33 p.m. on 8 December 1987. The president denied making policy decisions on such a basis, but his wife's press secretary confirmed that she regularly consulted 'a friend that does astrology'.

Modern education also makes space for such religious influences, especially in the field of management training. Courses aiming to develop 'self-awareness and personal fulfilment' are often heavy on religious concepts.

In *The New York Times* of 28 September 1986 there was a report of a meeting of executives from some of the world's largest multinationals, including IBM, AT&T and General Motors, to 'discuss how metaphysics, the occult and . . . mysticism might help executives compete in the world market'. These same ideas are also given credence in some of the West's leading universities. In Britain, even a conservative and traditional institution such as the University of Edinburgh has its professor of parapsychology. In the USA, the prestigious Divinity School of Harvard University offers courses on neo-paganism, and has hosted several conferences of witches. The Institute of Culture and Creation Spirituality at the Roman Catholic Holy Names College in Oakland, California, lists among its faculty a self-styled witch by the name of Starhawk.

Of course, there are several ways of understanding what all this means. Cynics want to regard it as fanciful make-believe, or even a marketing trick by those who want to make a fast buck. But there can be no denying that to many people it seems real enough for them to stake their lives on it. Millions in the West today are dissatisfied with what they have heard from traditional spiritual leaders in the Christian church, and are looking elsewhere for clear direction. More than ever before, our culture is in search of a new soul. A source of meaning and value. Something that will be worth believing in — and living for — as we face the dawn of a new millennium.

In 1900, something like 6 per cent of the world's population were self confessed atheists. Today that figure has shrunk to just a little over 4 per cent — of a vastly larger total world population! Fewer people than ever before are now inclined to deny the existence of something or somebody they can call 'God'. Every opinion poll for the last fifteen years has shown a steady increase in the level of religious belief. In Britain — supposedly one of the least religious Western nations (certainly by US standards) — about four-fifths of the population believe in God. On top of that, another 9 per cent describe themselves as agnostics: they don't know what to believe about the God question, but would be open to persuasion. That makes almost 90 per cent who either believe in God or would be open to do so given the right time and place.

In addition, more than 60 per cent of Britons can point to an occasion in their lives when they had what they would define as a 'religious experience'. Remember too that about 80 per cent of British homes own a Bible, and roughly the same number of people mark the great turning-points of life — birth, death, puberty and marriage — with a religious ceremony.

The picture is no different in the US. Almost 70 per cent believe in extra-sensory perception (ESP). One in four believe in reincarnation — almost one in three of under-thirties. And 42 per cent claim to have been in touch with another state of consciousness.

In the light of all these facts, it is hard to understand why philosophers still regularly describe religion as 'marginal' to our culture. To say we are non-religious is clearly untrue. Sure, we are less committed to what goes on in the four walls of church buildings on Sunday mornings. But it would be totally misleading to use that as a reliable thermometer for taking the spiritual temperature of our age.

2

Back to our Roots

To understand this interest in religion, let me take you back to our roots. To see where we have come from will help us to appreciate more clearly where we are now — and where we might yet be as we approach the twenty-first century. So join me on a quick trip down memory lane. Not my personal memory, of course — but the corporate memory of those who have gone before us and laid the foundations of Western civilization as we know it today. The eighteenth-century German diplomat Friedrich von Schlegel once remarked that 'a historian is a prophet in reverse'. There is a lot of truth in that. Being aware of our past can help us to be better equipped to deal with the present and the future. And nowhere is this more true than in thinking about religion.

A century ago, Karl Marx pronounced that 'Religion is the opium of the people'. At the time, he took it for granted that once people realized this, they would abandon religion once and for all. The facts are otherwise. Even in the USSR, religion has not only survived but flourishes. In 1949 there were about three quarters of a million Protestant Christians in China. They now number more than 4 million according to the government — perhaps up to ten times more, according to some sources.

As far back as we can go, it has always been that way. If Marx was right, then religion must be the most potent and seductive narcotic the world has ever known. In every civilization since time began, men and women have been intoxicated by it. Archaeologists and scholars often dig up the unexpected — but one thing they always find is evidence of religious beliefs and rituals. Right from the very dawn of history, people have found that everyday life makes most sense when it is viewed in the light of some being who can be called 'God'. Humans seem to have an in-built compulsive need to explain how things are by reference to something or someone who is either outside and beyond it all, or somehow embodied in the natural world. Wherever we look, it is impossible to understand people without understanding their religious faith. Occasionally, religion has led men and women to dazzling heights of moral achievement. Not infrequently, religion has inspired the most unimaginable cruelty. It has transformed the worst of people into saints and turned some of the best into demons. It can with justice be both praised and damned. But we cannot get away from it.

Even if we are not 'religious' ourselves, we all live in a culture which owes a great deal to those who were. The basic foundation of the Western way of life was constructed from the beliefs and purposes of Christianity. The Bible has had a formative influence in the evolution of our legal systems, our morals, our concepts of human rights, and our education. Like it or not, none of us can escape from its pervasive influence.

Almost 2,000 years ago, the Latin author Petronius, a one-time courtier in the palace of Nero, wrote that 'the gods walk abroad so commonly in our streets that it is easier to meet a god than a man'. Even today's package tourist can see what he meant, for Rome is jammed with religious sites of all descriptions. Churches, temples, cemeteries and shrines — they all bear witness to a city which has seen many different forms of religious enthusiasm and devotion. By any standards, Rome is an outstanding example of how religion can shape a civilization. But it is not unique. Faith in some sort of divine being had been around for thousands of years, long before this city became the centre of a mighty empire.

In the ancient Middle East, the very cradle of civilization, religious faith often began with questions and observations about the natural world. Take Mesopotamia, the area around the Persian Gulf. Life here depended on the two great rivers Tigris and Euphrates. They brought fertility to the fields, food to the people — and a means of transport. Further west, in Egypt, there was another great centre of ancient civilization. Here too men and women understood the meaning of life by reference to the river, which was the source of their economic prosperity. As the Nile rose and fell in an annual cycle it left in its wake a great covering of rich and fertile soil. Between these two ancient superpowers, in the traditional lands of the Bible, survival also depended on natural phenomena — this time on the rains coming at the right time in the year, and in the correct quantities.

Traditional Roman religion was also based on respect for the natural world, and natural forces such as rain, thunder and the sun were personified and worshipped. The Greeks had similar beliefs, which is why it was a simple matter for the traditional pantheon of Roman gods — Jupiter, Juno, Minerva, Mars, and others — to be identified with the Greek deities headed by Zeus. Everything found its true meaning by reference to the actions of these divine beings. If things went wrong, and the crops failed to mature — or if brave warriors were defeated in battle — neglect of the gods was the usual cause. Even simple everyday things like rain had a religious explanation: according to the Greek Strepsiades it meant that Zeus was pissing through a sieve!

But by the start of the Christian era a change had begun. Pressure for greater sophistication had been building up for many years. As far back as the fifth century BC serious thinkers in Athens had begun to question many of the old certainties. People were less content to accept what had come down to them from the mythology of the past. They questioned the long-established rules of morality and religion, and they were determined to have a reasoned explanation of things. They demanded hard evidence to back up popular beliefs, and where there seemed to be none they claimed the right to reject the beliefs.

The most outstanding surviving example of this new spirit of enquiry is to be found in the various works of the philosopher Plato (428-347BC). But its practical outworking can be seen in most Greek literature of the period: the history writing of Thucydides, the plays of Euripides and the comedies of Aristophanes. It led to a great expansion of knowledge not only about human behaviour but also about the natural world. Geology, astronomy, biology, mathematics and physics were all eagerly explored by great thinkers. Of course, not all their findings stood the test of time, and a modern scientist would laugh at the suggestion that the world's primary constituent was fire or water. But the discoveries of the new thinkers widened the horizons of many people, and led to a growing confidence in the power of human reason to resolve some of the big questions of human existence.

By the time the Roman Empire came on the scene, most educated people had been trained in one or other of the popular schools of philosophy. Ordinary people never went to school, and could make little sense of the speculations of the experts. But they knew enough to understand that things could never be quite the same again. The thinkers had apparently disproved the existence of the old traditional gods. And, in any case, new movements of trade and people were beginning to make Europeans more conscious of the fact that in other parts of the world other gods and goddesses were worshipped. Did they really exist? And if they did, how could they relate to life in the great urban centres of Greece and Italy?

The cradle of Christianity

All these uncertainties eventually led to a religious crisis in the Roman world. The philosophers had discredited traditional ways of explaining life. But they had failed to establish a plausible alternative. As a result, many people found themselves in a moral and spiritual vacuum. New ideas soon came rushing in to fill the void, especially from the East.

The 'mystery religions' were among the most popular. Mithraism, the soldier's religion, was one of them. But there were many others. They were all connected to the gods of Asia Minor (modern Turkey) and Egypt, and were called 'mysteries' because they were secret societies, whose members were sworn to say nothing about the rites in which they engaged. But many of them were based on the traditional fertility religions of the ancient Middle East. These mythologies originally explained the cycle of the seasons, as the new life of spring followed the barrenness of winter. Why did it happen like that? The usual answer was that the seasons changed as the gods of fertility died and were subsequently reborn. This was often celebrated in annual festivals at which male and female priests would act out the life cycle of the gods, usually ending with sexual acts which would guarantee the fertility of fields and flocks for the coming season.

In the new mystery religions, it was not just nature that could experience death and rebirth: individual worshippers could now share in the same mystical experience. Access to this experience was usually through an initiation ceremony. One account tells how the subject was placed in a pit in the ground, covered with a wicker framework. A bull — symbol of life and virility — would then be slaughtered on this framework, so that its blood ran down and soaked the initiate below. No doubt there were many such rituals, often combined with sexual rites too. Those who were initiated into such mysteries gained a new sense of hope and security, and personal meaning and purpose in life. They also found themselves part of a distinctive group of like-minded people who would give mutual support in times of need.

Judaism was also popular in the Roman world. Unlike the mysteries, it was easy to see what it was all about. Its ancient scriptures were widely available to be read in Greek, the common language of the empire. In addition there were Jewish communities in every major city of the Mediterranean world, so prospective converts could see for themselves what it involved. It frequently offered an attractive alternative to thinking people who were dissatisfied with the permissive morality of their own culture. As a result, many Greeks and Romans — especially of the educated classes — adopted the Jewish faith.

But more than anything else, this was the world in which Christianity came to birth. Jesus himself never travelled beyond his own native land of Palestine, but his followers soon took his message into the wider Roman world. Within twenty years of his death, there were thriving Christian communities in all the major centres of the Mediterranean lands, and the church grew very fast indeed. The Christian message had an obvious appeal for those who were part of the many Jewish communities — for it claimed to be the fulfilment and continuation of Judaism itself. But it also found many converts among adherents of the mystery religions. For Jesus too had spoken of a new supernatural power that could give meaning to the lives of ordinary people. And, like the mystery religions, Christianity gave believers access to a network of mutual support and social benefits in the life of local churches.

From such small and humble beginnings, Christianity came to dominate the religious scene in Europe for the remainder of Roman history, and on through the next millennium and a half. Long before the time of Jesus, the Greek philosopher Protagoras had declared that 'Man is the measure of all things', but most people found that hard to accept. The majority still preferred religious answers to life's great questions. And when the emperor himself, Constantine, became a Christian in AD312, the essential religious foundation of Western culture was laid down for generations to come. With only a few minor hiccups things were to continue virtually unchanged right through until the fifteenth and sixteenth centuries.

The way most ordinary people understood life and its meaning was simple: God was all powerful, up there in his heaven, looking after things on this earth, which was thought of as a flat disc. Underneath it was the world of the dead, usually depicted as a place of fiery punishment — hell — a place to avoid if at all possible. Avoiding it was a matter of being faithful to the church, to pre-empt the possibility that an angry God might send you there at death. Most things that happened from day to day could be traced back to God — or if not to him, then to the personification of evil, the devil, or one of his minions. In this kind of world-view, everything hung together. Religion permeated the whole of life. And life made sense only in the light of religion.

The self-confidence of this Christian Europe was challenged from time to time. A particularly serious confrontation came from the growing religion of Islam. Beginning in Mecca about AD610, it soon became a powerful force, especially at the eastern end of the Mediterranean Sea. Within little more than a hundred years, Muslim expansion had swept Christianity out of its original strongholds in North Africa, and even made inroads into France and Spain. For the next three centuries, Islamic influence was consolidated in the Middle East, and when the holy sites of Palestine were taken over and Byzantium, the Eastern capital of Christianity, was itself threatened, Western Christians decided to do something about it. A group of West European rulers, among them several kings of England, embarked on the Crusades — holy wars designed to push back what they saw as a pagan menace. They achieved little of lasting value. But the way in which kings of different countries were able to work hand in hand was a tribute to the remarkable sense of West European solidarity at this time.

Light in the darkness

The Crusades had shown that it was possible for Europeans to extend their influence many hundreds of miles away from their own native soil. It was not long before visionaries began wondering what other challenges were to be discovered just over the horizon. A new age of scientific investigation was about to dawn. Travellers such as Christopher Columbus (1451-1506) began to put new theories to the test. If the earth was, as some were now saying, not flat but round, then it must be possible to sail westwards and reach the East! And before long the Portuguese explorer Ferdinand Magellan did just that. These were stirring and exciting times in which to live. In this great age of discovery, the shape of the world was — quite literally — redrawn. New lands and unexpected people were discovered for the first time by European explorers.

There were also many other areas of knowledge where fresh facts were coming to light. Sir Isaac Newton wondered why apples always fall downwards and not up — and thought of the law of gravity to explain it. Others began to watch the moon and the stars, and formulated ideas about the workings of the solar system. In the process they discovered that our earth is not, after all, the centre of it all, but just one tiny and insignificant part of something far more vast.

No wonder people were soon referring to this period of history as the 'Enlightenment'. For that is just what it was. Compared with the new discoveries, the old world of the Middle Ages and before seemed like darkness — full of superstition and ignorance. Whereas then people had felt their lives to be hemmed in by cosmic forces they could do little about, now new possibilities seemed to stretch out endlessly before them. Though there were still many uncertainties, it finally seemed as if people might be able to control their environment, rather than the environment controlling them. Great voyages of discovery became commonplace, and with them the imperialistic Britain and other Western powers expanded into virtually every part of the globe. These were heady days, when it seemed that nothing was impossible to achieve.

Moreover, as people reflected on all their new-found know-ledge, it seemed that God had little to do with it. The new discoveries had not come through some divine revelation from outside: they were the result of sheer hard work, and the applica-tion of human brainpower. Many of the old beliefs about religion, about manners and customs, began to look fairly arbitrary, and as a result thinking people began to take them less seriously. People became less likely to accept the rules and explanations handed down to them by their fathers. They wanted to know the reasons behind everything, and to justify and examine things for themselves. If people had the freedom to decide what to eat or what to wear, why should they not make their own choice about what is right and wrong too? The same with religion. They demanded evidence for traditional beliefs, and if none could be produced then they were inclined to reject the beliefs. A rediscovery of the classics of Greece and Rome added further impetus to this enquiring spirit. For these were exactly the kind of questions that had been asked 400 years before Christ's birth by the philosophers of ancient Athens.

The discoveries of this period changed the face of European culture once and for all. In science, geography, medicine and many other fields of knowledge amazing things were happening — of which we today are major beneficiaries. Instead of vague speculations about how the world works, systematic and informed thinking was able to discover how it really is. Ignorance became a thing of the past, and there seemed to be nothing that could not be fully explained merely by the application of human reason. Even the world itself seemed to work in predictable ways once the 'laws of nature' were properly understood.

In the face of such confidence in human brainpower, religion had a hard time. Paradoxically, it was religion that, to some extent, encouraged the rationalism that led to its own collapse. For the Protestant Reformation had encouraged people to read the Bible for themselves and to draw their own conclusions about it, instead of blindly believing what the church said. The Reformers, of course, had found in the Bible a different way of understanding God than the received wisdom of the medieval Catholic church. But who could argue that if others now wanted to read it and make no sense of God at all, they were not fully entitled to their opinions?

As a result the Bible — and Christian faith along with it — was gradually marginalized for most serious thinkers. Instead of going to the Bible to find out how the world was made, or how we should behave, people looked instead to the theories of scientists and philosophers. They were the ones who claimed to understand things as they actually are, rather than as some religious visionary imagined they might be. The unified world-view of people in the Middle Ages, for whom religion was a natural part of everyday life, was smashed beyond repair. Opinion-formers declared that from then on the only valid way to get at the real facts about how life is would be by the intellectual endeavour of thinking people. If religion had a place at all in this new world, it was marginal — though most agreed that no real harm would be done if those who were interested in such things followed it in their spare time.

And the Bible? In this new climate of thought, that too could be little more than an interesting collection of opinions. Influential opinions, perhaps — but just one possible set out of many, and certainly not the absolute truth. How could a book so ancient — written in an age of darkness, ignorance and superstition — possibly be relevant to the lives of people in a world which had witnessed so many amazing breakthroughs in science and technology?

These were understandable questions. Who was it who initially opposed the idea that the earth might be round? Christians, of course. And why did they argue that way? Because they claimed the Bible taught that the earth was flat! We can hardly be surprised then that rationalist thinkers concluded that the Bible could no longer make sense to modern people. That seemed like stating the obvious. And since no Christians at the time had any convincing arguments to the contrary, most people came to believe that 'science' had disproved it — a view that is still widely held even today.

New questions for the New Age

We have all reaped enormous benefits from the pioneering thinkers of the Enlightenment. No one would wish to go back to the days when people thought the earth was flat, and when every simple illness was imagined to be the result of demon possession. The improvements brought into all our lives by the ongoing discoveries in medicine and technology are plain to see. And they continue.

But there is a tarnished side to the golden coin of modern progress. For in the heady optimism of the eighteenth and nineteenth centuries, people genuinely believed that with a clearer understanding of how things are we would also be able to control the future, to produce a better world for ourselves and our children. Rational people, behaving rationally in a predictable world that operated according to fixed laws of nature, would automatically ensure harmony and happiness for the human race. People have always recognized that a satisfying life depends on certain basic qualities. Peace, security, good health, long life, living in harmony with nature — these are some of the more obviously desirable things. In some respects, we have made considerable progress. In the developed world, we can expect to live more healthily, and for longer, than our grandparents, thanks to the advances of medical science.

But we also know that is not the whole story. For people in the impoverished Two-Thirds World, life is often quite different. In many places a child who reaches the age of five is fortunate indeed. And when we look to some of our other basic aspirations, then the record of supposedly 'enlightened' thinkers begins to look decidedly shaky. Notwithstanding its undoubted benefits, modern science has a dark side to it. Without nuclear physicists, the world would never have known the weapons of mass destruction whose devastating potential terrifies us all. Even without them, we have to reckon with the brutal realities of two world wars in the first half of the twentieth century.

The optimistic idealists of the nineteenth century fondly imagined that as we became more knowledgeable we would also become better. But the facts prove almost the exact opposite. As we approach the end of the twentieth century, it is unsafe to walk in the streets of many of our cities. Muggings and rapes are so commonplace as to be normal. Child abuse has reached epidemic proportions. Millions are starving all over the world. We have even caused irreparable damage to the earth itself. Many species of birds and animals are extinct. Many more soon will be. Rivers and seas are polluted beyond recovery. And the greenhouse effect may yet fry us alive in our own lifetime — unless we exterminate ourselves by some other means first. Being able to understand what is going on seems to make little difference to either our capacity to cope with it, or to change things. For many it simply compounds their misery.

When the history of our time comes to be written, the 1980s will be seen as the decade when ordinary people woke up to the truth of our situation, and began to question the confident assumptions of Enlightenment thinkers. If the truth is to be found through human reason, and if we are even half as clever as we think we are, then why is life still so unpredictable and unsatisfactory for so many people?

That imponderable question has sparked off the new religious quest of Western culture. Abstract intellectual answers no longer satisfy. The Enlightenment taught us to think of life in a purely mechanistic way. Everything is a matter of cause and effect. The world works that way, controlled by unchanging 'laws of nature'. But the facts of modern living seem to suggest it is not that simple.

At a very basic level, many can now see the inadequacy of all this in the way that conventional medicine has handled its patients. Frequently they are treated as if they are no more than dead bodies that happen to be still breathing. Most of us feel dehumanized by such attitudes, for the truth is that the human person is a complex bundle of emotions and feelings as well — not to mention the 'spiritual' dimension of which many are aware. As a result, thousands today search for personal healing in 'alternative' medicine, choosing the apparently 'unscientific' techniques of Chinese acupuncture and Eastern meditation in preference to Western medical science.

But there is more to it than a sense of personal alienation. Henry Ford was one of the most successful entrepreneurs of the twentieth century. Born in middle America in 1863, by the time he was forty he had founded the Ford Motor Company. Twenty years later he was turning out 2 million cars a year, at prices that made them accessible for the first time to ordinary people. By the time of his death in 1947, he was recognized the world over as an outstanding example of the self-made man. And what was the secret of his success? In a famous interview published in the *Chicago Tribune* on 25 May 1916, he was quoted as saying:

What do we care what they did 500 or 1000 years ago? It means nothing to me. History is more or less bunk. It's tradition. We don't want tradition. We want to live in the present and the only history that is worth a tinker's dam is the history we make today. That's the trouble with the world. We're living in books and history and tradition.

We want to get away from that and take care of today. We've done too much looking back. What we want to do, and do it quick, is to make just history right now.

They were provocative words, but they captured the mood of many people at the time. In fact they caused such a stir that Ford later sued the newspaper for libel. And when he was quizzed in court about his alleged statements that 'books, history and tradition' caused all the trouble in the world, he contented himself with the less flamboyant observation: 'Never served me very much purpose'.

If anything, more people would agree with him today than in his own generation. Life moves at such a pace, with technology propelling us into ever more fantastic frontiers of knowledge and experience, that the only thing worth living for seems to be today and tomorrow. Inspired by modern psychoanalysts such as Freud and Jung, and the sociologist Abraham Maslow who identified 'self-actualisation' as the ultimate human goal, many are abandoning the heritage of our past to seek more immediate relief for the world's problems. Discontent with modern scientific achievement has rubbed off on to everything that comes from the past — including the traditional Christian philosophy on which our civilization was based.

A new beginning

When in the mid-sixties the theme song from the rock musical *Hair* proclaimed 'This is the Age of Aquarius', it was announcing a new beginning. Aquarius is the eleventh sign of the ancient zodiac, otherwise known as 'the water-bearer' — hence an appropriate symbol for a new age of liberation in which the long-standing thirst for truth would finally be quenched. Many would say that Christianity, with its view of a God who is all powerful and almighty, has failed. In a world where little seems to make sense, alternative philosophies are eagerly embraced in the desperate search for personal meaning. New answers are drawn from a variety of sources, including great world religions such as Hinduism and Buddhism, as well as ancient systems such as Gnosticism and the Roman mystery religions.

Millions of people around the world see this as the pathway to a better life. They talk of the world as being on the verge of something as profound as the Reformation or the Enlightenment itself. The old order is about to give way to a new era of peace, prosperity and perfection. In the final years of the second millennium, many are looking for some event of world-shattering significance.

In 1982 Maharishi Mahesh Yogi, founder of Transcendental Meditation (TM), announced he was setting up a centre for each million people on earth, each one with a TM teacher for every 1,000 people in the population. As soon as 1 per cent of the population practices TM, he believes, the world will be saved from war and strife.

George King, the English-born leader of the Aetherius Society based in Los Angeles but with branches throughout the world, claims to have been contacted by many Extra-Terrestrial Intelligences, including 'Master Jesus', and he predicts that a 'New Master' will arrive 'shortly and openly . . . in a Flying Saucer'.

Others expect the arrival soon of 'the cleansing', a time when the very universe itself will rebel against modern technology and the damage it has done to the earth.

And, for good measure, some fundamentalist Christians see 'new age' thinking like this as itself a sign that the end of the world is at hand!

It would be foolish to deny that our world is in a mess. But is this radical change of direction the only possible solution? Is it really true that the Bible and its message has created our present problems? And if not, what is the Bible saying to us? Can we trust it anyway? And how can a book so ancient make sense 2,000 years after its last page was written? These are some of the questions we will explore in what follows.

Christians can afford to ignore these issues no longer. They are crucial for the continued survival not only of the church but also for Western culture in the form it has hitherto taken.

But more than that, they are vital questions for anyone who is searching for personal fulfilment, and a meaningful answer to the world's present crisis. For the Bible is by any standards a remarkable book. If it is right when it claims that Jesus is 'the truth', it demands to be taken seriously by us all — and we ignore it at our peril.

3

Is the Bible a Hoax?

The Bible's most recent parts were written something like 2,000 years ago — yet it is still the world's number one bestseller. It has been translated into more languages than any other book, and has had a profound influence on the whole history of civilization. Men and women have died for the privilege of being able to read it. And even today, millions of people throughout the world avidly read it as a source of personal inspiration for daily living.

But most Westerners are in two minds about it. In Britain, for example, 80 per cent of homes possess a Bible, but hardly anyone — including church members — seems to read it at all consistently. And while most of us evidently respect its message — especially the teaching of Jesus — we also frequently treat the Bible with a good deal of suspicion. Hasn't science somehow 'disproved' it, we ask? Was it not tampered with back in the early centuries of the Christian era, to make it say what orthodox Christians wanted it to say? And in its original form did it not give credence to notions such as reincarnation which the church has traditionally rejected?

Some ask such questions with a serious purpose — as when Muslims claim that the stories of Jesus in the New Testament Gospels tell only half the truth. Other claims verge on the unbelievable. Like the sensational theories of novelist Erich von Daniken who proposed that the Bible originally contained stories of visits to our planet by UFOs and ETIs, and that these stories were all doctored by the early Church Fathers back in the second and third centuries!

Most of us have also come across vague claims that there were 'other books' that didn't quite make it into the Bible. And when such rejected writings allegedly contain versions of the teaching of Jesus and his disciples that seem fundamentally different from what is in the Bible, then we naturally begin to wonder what is going on.

We will tackle all these questions in due course. In this chapter, we make a start by looking at the business of authenticity. The various books of the Bible were written over a long period of time, beginning more than a thousand years before the birth of Jesus and ending perhaps seventy or eighty years after his death. The books of the Old Testament — originally the Bible of the Jewish faith — were mostly written in Hebrew, with just a handful of pages in another similar language, Aramaic. The New Testament documents were written entirely in Greek, the international language of the Roman Empire at the time. The original manuscripts of all these books have long since perished. There is no such thing as a 'first edition' of the Bible, and no one knows what happened to the actual sheets on which its books were first written down. Probably they did not last beyond the generation in which they were produced.

Even as long ago as the time of Jesus, the Hebrew Bible was known only through copies of copies, stretching back in a continuous line into the dim and distant past. In this respect, the Bible is no worse off than any other literature from the ancient world. We have no originals of the classics of ancient Greece and Rome either. Nor, for that matter, of the Quran or the Baghavadgita. But these facts pose some crucial questions for today's readers. How can we know that the Bible in our hands is what its original authors intended it to be? Can we trust it? And where has it come from?

Searching for ancient manuscripts

You would hardly expect words like detective story or treasure hunt to be used in connection with the Bible. Yet when you look at the way some of the ancient documents have come to light, that kind of language seems entirely appropriate. For me, the search began one cold winter afternoon in the University of Glasgow, Scotland. Not the most obvious place to look, perhaps, but the library there contains a remarkable collection of books and papers gathered together by one of the world's most adventurous collectors of ancient manuscripts.

Constantin von Tischendorf was a professor at the University of Leipzig in Germany in the nineteenth century. When he died in 1874 the trustees of Trinity College in Glasgow got the chance to buy his library. It cost them the grand sum of £460, an amount which they raised first from their own donations, and then by an appeal to the Free Church Assembly in May 1877. The Assembly commended the collection to its people in glowing terms:

For this most interesting acquisition the Glasgow college and the Free Church are especially indebted to the zeal and energy of Professor Lindsay. He has also collected a large part of the amount required: and it is hoped that wealthy friends in the west will not leave him in anxiety as to the balance. There is no respect in which a wise munificence may be better exercised than in enabling our college libraries to acquire rare and valuable books beyond the reach of private individuals, and scarcely to be found in any of our public libraries.

No one seems to know how Professor Lindsay came across the papers. But he must have had plenty of wealthy friends, for they raised the cash required to buy them in double-quick time, and the Tischendorf collection found a permanent home in his college. From the fine words of the General Assembly you might have expected that these books would have been given pride of place. In fact they were left locked away in a library cupboard, uncatalogued and all but forgotten, for the next hundred years. Then in 1974, when Trinity College had fallen into such a state of disrepair that it was almost collapsing, they were rediscovered and presented to the University of Glasgow.

They tell a fascinating story that starts in 1839 with the young Tischendorf twenty-four years old. Five years earlier he had gone to the University of Leipzig, where he developed a keen fascination for the New Testament. He decided to try to reconstruct its text in the exact words that its authors had originally written. He started work with such materials as he could find in Leipzig. But he soon realized that to make much progress he would need to travel. Many of the great libraries of Europe had lain undisturbed for centuries, and Tischendorf had a hunch that if he could get into some of them he would be able to unearth Bible manuscripts and other materials that had been ignored or forgotten for generations.

As it turned out, his initial dreams were to be fulfilled beyond his greatest expectations. But like many great scholars and explorers, Tischendorf was not particularly well off. So his first job was to persuade other, richer people that he was worth supporting. He started with his own government, and they gave him a grant of

100 thalers to cover his travelling expenses. When you consider that for 5 thalers you could buy a whole week's groceries, you might be forgiven for thinking that this was a generous grant. But Tischendorf was not impressed. He wrote in his diary:

What was such a sum as this with which to undertake a long journey? Full of faith, however, in the proverb that 'God helps those who help themselves', and that what is right must prosper, I resolved, in 1840, to set out for Paris . . . though I had not sufficient means to pay even for my travelling suit; and when I reached Paris I had only 50 thalers left. The other fifty had been spent on my journey.

Once in Paris, Tischendorf was soon caught up in an argument that would win him fame and, more importantly, fortune. It all started with a document which he found in the National Library of Paris. It appeared to be a copy of the writings of St Ephraem, a fourth-century leader of the Syrian church. But on close examination, it turned out to have more than one layer of writing on it. Good writing material was very valuable in the ancient world, especially if it was made of leather as was this one. Instead of buying new materials all the time, enterprising scribes made a habit of taking redundant documents, scrubbing them clean, and then using them over again. This is what had happened here — and the experts in Paris were trying to decipher the writing that had been there originally before it was scrubbed off.

They had tried everything — strong lights, chemicals, and other weird ideas — but with no success. Eventually they declared it would be impossible to read what was underneath. But they had reckoned without Tischendorf's determination. Since he was interested in such documents, he thought he had nothing to lose by taking a look at this one. After many hours of hard work — and, presumably, good eyesight — he not only deciphered the original writing, but was also able to determine the document's history. It had, he said, been written to begin with in the fifth century, and then renovated in the seventh century and again in the ninth — finally to be scrubbed clean and inscribed with different material in the twelfth century.

The scholars in Paris were amazed by this extraordinary discovery. Tischendorf became a hero overnight — and with this success behind him he had no difficulty in raising very substantial funds for his other projects. Well-to-do patrons of the arts were so impressed, they were falling over themselves to have their names associated with his. But what interested Tischendorf most was that the writing he had uncovered on this mysterious manuscript was an ancient copy of parts of the Bible. He began to wonder if other documents like this existed elsewhere. He wrote:

The literary treasures which I have sought to explore have been drawn in most cases from the convents of the east where, for ages, the pens of industrious monks have copied the sacred writings, and collected manuscripts of all kinds. It therefore occurred to me whether it was not probable that in some recess of Greek or Coptic, Syrian or Armenian monasteries, there might be some precious manuscripts sheltering for ages in dust and darkness.

With this possibility in mind, he set off on an epic journey to scour the monasteries of the East. Little did he realize what an astounding voyage of discovery it was going to be.

He began by going round all the great European centres of learning — Venice, Modena, Milan, Verona, Turin, Rome — searching their libraries for ancient manuscripts. And he made many significant discoveries. In Florence he came across a copy of the Bible translated into Latin by the fourth-century Italian scholar Jerome in a cave in Bethlehem. But it had travelled hundreds of miles before it found a home in northern Italy.

Its journey had begun at Jarrow, in the north of England — a place which in the seventh and eighth centuries was one of the great cultural and religious centres of Western Europe. It was here that the Venerable Bede wrote his *Ecclesiastical History of the English People* — and here too that he made a start on translating the Bible into Anglo-Saxon. He translated from Latin, and may conceivably have known the very manuscript Tischendorf discovered. It was during Bede's lifetime that the abbot of his monastery decided to make a pilgrimage to Rome, taking this document with him as a suitable gift for the pope. Neither the abbot nor his gift ever arrived. For he died on the journey, and the manuscript found a home in the Italian monastery of Monte Amiata in the northern Alps. There it remained for 1,000 years, until the monastery itself closed in 1782, and the manuscript was taken to Florence. That was where Tischendorf found it eighty years later, and told the world about it.

But it was on the second leg of his epic journey that he made his greatest find. In April 1844 he moved on to the Bible lands — Egypt, Libya, Arabia and Palestine. Here, at the remote site of one of the great events of Bible history, Constantin von Tischendorf was to make history himself. Beneath the rocky crags of Mt Sinai, where God gave Moses the Ten Commandments, he came upon the stern walls of St Catherine's monastery:

It was at the foot of Mount Sinai, in the convent of St Catherine, that I discovered the pearl of all my researches. In visiting the library of the monastery, in the month of May 1844, I perceived in the middle of the great hall a large and wide basket full of old parchments; and the librarian, who was a man of information, told me that two heaps of papers like these, mouldered by time, had already been committed to the flames.

As Tischendorf thumbed through these pages, he saw that they contained parts of the Old Testament in Greek. And as he compared them with the Greek Old Testament he already knew, he realized that these were the most ancient copies he had ever seen. He tried to persuade the monks to give him all the pages, but they became suspicious and would only let him have those sheets that were about to be burned — forty-three of them in all. But at least he managed to persuade them not to destroy any more until he could return to study the whole manuscript in greater detail.

Once he got back to Europe, he was kept busy sorting and cataloguing the other documents he had found on his travels. But he could not stop thinking about the manuscript at the foot of Mt Sinai. He kept in touch with the monks through a friend at the Egyptian royal court. But even with friends in such high places he was unable to secure the precious pages. In desperation, he decided to return to the monastery and laboriously copy the entire document out by hand. So in 1853, nine years after his first visit, he once more knocked on the door of the monastery. He was well received by the monks, and was shown many of their treasures. But he could find no trace of the manuscript that had impressed him so much before. To his great disappointment, he was forced to return to Europe empty-handed.

Then he thought of a better plan. This time, he would get the backing of the Russian government.

It was a wise move, for the monks of St Catherine's belonged to the Orthodox church, and regarded the Russian emperor as the patron and protector of their faith. But there were other obstacles to overcome first:

This proposal only aroused a jealous and fanatical opposition in St Petersburg. People were astonished that a foreigner and a Protestant should presume to ask the support of the emperor of the Greek and Orthodox church for a mission to the east. But the good cause triumphed. The interest which my proposal excited, even within the imperial circle, inclined the emperor in my favour.

In January 1859, with the backing of the Russian emperor, Tischendorf set out once again for Mt Sinai. It was to be a momentous journey. He was given a great welcome by the monks — and at long last he discovered the whereabouts of the priceless manuscript he had first glimpsed fifteen years before:

Full of joy, which this time I had the self-command to conceal from the steward and the rest of the community, I asked, as if in a careless way, for permission to take the manuscript into my sleeping chamber to look over it more at leisure. There by myself I could give way to the transport of joy which I felt. I knew that I held in my hand the most precious Biblical treasure in existence . . .

After lengthy and delicate negotiations, which took him all the way from Egypt to Constantinople and back, it was agreed that Tischendorf should take the whole manuscript to Russia to have it copied and examined as carefully as possible. Finally, back in Russia, on 19 November 1859, he presented it to Alexander II, along with plans for its publication. Tischendorf himself was to be the editor, and when the work was finished his enterprise and scholarship was acclaimed by the whole world. The emperor of Russia sent copies of it far and wide, and Tischendorf received honours from the pope and other religious leaders, as well as degrees from Oxford and Cambridge universities in England. When he was presented to these ancient universities, one British scholar commented somewhat enviously: 'I would rather have discovered this Sinaitic manuscript than the crown jewels of the queen of England.' It was that important.

He was not the only one to recognize its value. In the 1930s the Soviet government decided to get rid of Tischendorf's treasure, and the British government forked out £100,000 to buy it. This was a huge sum in those days, and its arrival in the British Museum at Christmas 1933 was one of the great events of the thirties.

. . . the queue of those desirous of passing in front of it was continuous . . . the crowd appeared to be drawn from all sorts and conditions of men and women, and to be of many nations and languages. As they appeared within sight of the shining parchment sheets, not a few were moved out of reverence to take off their hats. While none could linger for more than a few seconds before the glass case, some passed by quicker than others; for the majority a look was enough, and they departed in peace . . .

That was how the London *Times* reported the affair, and Tischendorf would have appreciated its language. For he too was convinced that in this document he had encountered more than just another old Bible. Writing of it later, he reflected:

While so much had been lost in the course of centuries, by the tooth of time or by the carelessness of ignorant monks, an invisible eye had watched over this treasure and when it was on the point of perishing in the fire, the Lord had decreed its deliverance.

Few, if any, modern scholars would feel moved to this kind of mystical reverence for his discovery. But there can be no doubt of its importance. Tischendorf's beloved *Codex Sinaiticus* (as it came to be known) was laying the foundations for the most accurate text of the New Testament ever known. The train of events that his discovery set in motion was to extend far beyond his own time — even beyond his own century, and into our own. The manuscript turned out to have been written — in Greek — about the middle of the fourth century AD, and to contain all the New Testament as well as a few sections of the Old. It is still the most complete ancient Bible manuscript that we have.

But it is not the oldest. Not by a long way. To find that we must turn our attention to another momentous discovery, this one much nearer to our own time. Tischendorf went looking for ancient manuscripts. He knew what he was searching for, and had a fair idea where to look. But advances in knowledge just as often come about by accident. This was what happened with the famous Dead Sea Scrolls.

Spectacular discoveries

In spring 1947 a young Arab shepherd by the name of Jum'a Muhammed was wandering along the foot of the cliffs that overlook the north-eastern shore of the Dead Sea. To him and his companions it was just another day, and the only business in hand was to ensure that their flocks of sheep and goats managed to find enough grazing to satisfy their daily requirements. The people of their tribe — the Ta'amireh — had lived like this for generations, and they knew all the nooks and crannies of this barren and forbidding landscape. At least, they thought they did. But as he clambered over the cliffs in pursuit of a wandering animal, Jum'a noticed a couple of small holes in the sheer rock face, high above where he stood. With little else to do, he tossed a stone through one of the openings. To his surprise, instead of a dull thud as the stone landed in the cave, he thought he heard a sound of breaking pottery.

To hear pottery breaking in this most unexpected of places could mean only one thing: treasure of some sort. This was not a spot where great towns and cities had ever stood. But precisely because of its remoteness, several legends had become attached to it. The Old Testament 'city of salt', mentioned in Joshua chapter 15, was thought to be somewhere around here, and nineteenth-century archaeologists had looked for the remains of the biblical Gomorrah in this area. They found nothing of interest at the time. But breaking pottery in mysterious caves must mean something.

Jum'a soon decided that he would not be the one to go into the caves. At least, not by himself, for it was obvious that one cave was far too small, and the other was not much bigger. His two cousins were helping with the flocks, and one of them — Muhammed Ahmed el-Hamed — was only a teenager. He would have a better chance of getting in and — more important — back out of these inviting but intimidating vaults. But no one was in any great hurry, and it was two or three days before the three friends decided to settle their flocks overnight at the foot of the cliff just below the caves.

First thing next morning, the teenager was awake before the others. It was a long way up to the caves — a hundred metres and more. But it was not for nothing that he was nicknamed edh-Dhib, 'the wolf'. A lifetime's experience of chasing after wayward sheep and goats had taught him how to climb safely.

In no time at all, he had lowered himself into the higher of the two openings. Jum'a had originally imagined that there might be coins — even gold or jewels — hidden away in here. But edh-Dhib found only a few stone jars. Most of them were empty. A couple were full of dirt and rubbish. One contained a roll of old leather. Then there were two other packages wrapped in rotten green cloth. His older companions were glad they had not made the effort to rise early, if this was all there was to find. The bundles turned out to be documents of some kind, but in a script they did not understand. And their general condition hardly suggested they would be of much value. In fact, when they returned to their home base not far from Bethlehem, Jum'a casually hung them all up on the pole of his tent!

He soon had second thoughts, however, and over the next month or two various other items were removed from the caves, mostly more scrolls. They eventually found their way to the market in Bethlehem, where several traders had a regular business buying and selling such items. The dealers were initially suspicious, fearing that they had been stolen from a museum. But in due course their existence became public knowledge when they fell into the hands of Metropolitan Samuel of St Mark's Monastery in Jerusalem.

The exact sequence of events by which they got there is shrouded in mystery. But they soon sparked off a lively debate among those who knew about such things. Some experts unhesitatingly dated them at least as early as the first century BC. Others insisted they were medieval. One even declared them a modern forgery. But the tribespeople knew they were on to a good thing, and the caves above the Dead Sea soon became the place to go.

By now, the United Nations had announced the establishment of the Jewish state of Israel, and Palestine was thrown into disorder and conflict. No professional archaeologist had any hope of reaching the area around the Dead Sea. By the beginning of 1949, the Arab Legion had posted a guard on the caves, but by then dozens of unauthorized explorers had already been inside and had removed various items and left their own twentieth-century rubbish behind. Nevertheless, there were still many fragments of scrolls scattered about the caves, together with various jars and bits of cloth in which they had originally been contained. Analysis of these confirmed beyond any doubt that these scrolls and jars were even earlier than anyone had imagined, and dated from about 200-250BC, or possibly a little earlier.

Down on the plateau and less than a mile away were some ruins that had been known for a long time: Kirbet Qumran. In fact these had been superficially excavated by archaeologists in the middle of the nineteenth century. But now they assumed a new importance. Could these ruins be connected with the scrolls that were gradually emerging from the caves?

Thorough excavations in the early 1950s soon demonstrated that they were. The site had been occupied as long ago as the seventh and eighth centuries BC, but the major remains dated from the centuries immediately surrounding the beginning of the Christian era. Occupation finally ended in AD135, but the manuscripts were probably hidden just before AD70, the year when the Romans devastated Jerusalem itself. The ruins of Qumran show remarkable signs of the mechanical skills of those who lived here. To find enough water to drink in the middle of the desert was difficult enough. But these people constructed a complex system of aqueducts and cisterns, gathering water in enormous quantities, apparently for use in religious rituals as well as more ordinary things such as washing and drinking. Other remarkable finds include the remains of the tables at which the scrolls were first written — complete with ancient ink-wells, with the parched remnants of ink inside them!

These people were apparently Essenes, a Jewish religious group mentioned by several ancient writers. These particular Essenes had obviously chosen to live in an isolated monastic community, regarding themselves as a faithful remnant within the otherwise corrupt Jewish nation. But not all Essenes lived in this way, and they could be found throughout the country. The discovery of their monastery, and the scrolls, has led to many fascinating insights into the beliefs and way of life of this particular group. But the main interest for us lies in the scrolls themselves.

In the years following the initial discoveries, other caves in the area were systematically explored, and dozens more texts came to light. Among them were the rules of the community and many religious commentaries. There were also texts covering every book of the Hebrew Bible except one (Esther). Not all were complete manuscripts, of course. But some go back into the Old Testament period itself. There are scraps of the books of Samuel which are as old as the third century BC, and some of the texts of Daniel may have been written less than a hundred years after the book was first compiled. The most outstanding finds are very significant indeed. Like the Isaiah scroll, probably one of those first found by the three shepherds, which contains the complete Bible book of Isaiah. It is an enormous work, made out of seventeen sheets of leather sewn together side by side to make a scroll measuring almost 8 metres in length, by about 26 centimetres high. As well as this major find, there is also a second scroll of Isaiah, though that is incomplete and has suffered serious damage.

Before these momentous discoveries, the oldest texts of the Hebrew Bible were from the ninth and tenth centuries AD — supplemented by earlier copies of a Greek translation of the Old Testament that was made in Egypt just before the time of Jesus, but survives mostly in manuscripts from the third and fourth centuries AD. This is what Tischendorf found in the Old Testament section of his *Codex Sinaiticus*.

Thanks to the chance discovery of the Dead Sea Scrolls, we now have manuscripts in Hebrew that are a thousand years older than any known before. They reveal what scholars had always suspected — that there were several editions of the Old Testament in use at the time of Jesus. But all the differences between them were in relatively minor details — the sort of divergence that you would notice even between three or four English translations. Geza Vermes, one of the leading Jewish experts on the Scrolls writes:

With this newly discovered material at their disposal, experts concerned with the study of the text and transmission of the Scriptures are now able to achieve far greater accuracy in their deductions and can trace the process by which the text of the Bible attained its final shape. Moreover, they are in a position to prove that it has remained virtually unchanged for the last two thousand years.

Evidence for the Bible

What does all this prove about the text of the Bible? It means that we can say without hesitation that the text of the Bible as we know it is, in all essentials, identical with what its original authors wrote down.

Indeed, if we compare the Bible with other documents from the ancient world, then we have far more documentary and manuscript evidence for it than for any other book.

Take the works of Julius Caesar, for example. These were written in the first century BC. But there are less than a dozen surviving ancient manuscripts — and the oldest date from as late as AD800 to 900. The Histories of Tacitus are the same. Written towards the end of the first century AD, most of them are now lost — and our entire knowledge of what survives depends on only two manuscripts. And their dates? The ninth and the eleventh centuries AD respectively! Things are exactly the same in the case of classical Greek writers. The earliest complete manuscript of the work of Thucydides (460-400BC) dates from about AD900, and there are less than ten manuscripts in all. Compared with any of these, the Bible scores very highly on the issue of authenticity.

In addition to the great manuscripts whose story we have told in detail, there are thousands of others. For the New Testament, the very earliest is a scrap of papyrus now on display in John Rylands University Library in Manchester, England. It contains words from the Gospel of John, and was written about AD130, certainly less than a hundred years after the Gospel was written, and perhaps less than fifty.

Papyrus was widely used as writing material in the early Christian centuries. It was made from a plant which grew in the rivers and marshes of Egypt. The pith was cut into strips, which were then set out in two layers at right angles to one another so that the fibres were horizontal on one side and vertical on the other. The two layers were compressed together and dried to make sheets, which were then joined side by side to form a long strip of papyrus that could be rolled up. A convenient length for a roll would be about 11 metres, which was large enough to contain the longest of the Gospels. But the Christians soon found it was easier to fold papyrus sheets down the middle and sew them together like a modern book (a codex).

There are many large papyrus documents containing parts of the New Testament. In Dublin there is an extensive collection, including the Chester Beatty Papyri I and II. Number I contains parts of the Gospels and Acts, and number II has 86 almost perfectly preserved leaves of what was originally a book of 104 pages that contained all the letters of Paul. They were written between AD200 and 300. The Bodmer Library in Geneva also contains several such documents, including one of 108 pages which includes almost the whole of the first 14 chapters of John's Gospel, and dates from about AD200. Another Bodmer papyrus of similar age contains parts of Luke and John — while yet another has the letters of Peter and Jude.

Papyrus was a relatively unstable writing medium, for being of vegetable origin it soon went mouldy when exposed to damp. That is why most of the significant papyrus finds have been made in Egypt, where the dry atmosphere and hot desert sand provided ideal conditions for their preservation. Vellum or parchment was far more durable. This was made from the skins of animals, and by the first half of the fourth century AD it was widely used for all the best books. All the early surviving complete copies of the New Testament were made from vellum, and written in what is called uncial writing — a literary book style a bit like modern printed lettering. There are at least 250 of these biblical documents. *Codex Sinaiticus* we have already met, and it is one of the earliest (about AD350). *Codex Vaticanus*, which has been in the Vatican Library at Rome since 1431, dates from about the same time. It too was originally a complete Bible, but most of Genesis, some of the Psalms, the latter part of Hebrews, 1 and 2 Timothy, Titus, and Revelation have since disappeared.

There is also *Codex Alexandrinus*, which dates from the first half of the fifth century. It originally contained a complete Bible, though several sections have since been lost. Its name comes from the belief that it may have been written at Alexandria in Egypt. But it was presented to Charles I of England from Constantinople and has been in the British Museum in London since it was founded.

Codex Bezae is another fifth-century manuscript, with Greek and Latin texts on opposite pages. It contains only the Gospels and Acts, with a few passages of other New Testament books. No one knows where it was written, but it was bought at Lyons in France in 1562 by the scholar Beza, who presented it to Cambridge University. Then there is *Codex Ephraemi*, from the same period. This is the document which Tischendorf first deciphered in Paris. It too originally contained the whole Bible, but much of it has been lost. What remains, however, includes the whole New Testament apart from 2 Thessalonians and 2 John.

As if this were not enough, the Bible was also in constant use by Christians for worship and study from the very beginning of the Christian era. Before long it was being translated into many different languages, and we have countless ancient versions of the Bible, including Syriac, Coptic, Latin, Gothic, Armenian, Ethiopic and Arabic. A particularly interesting text is the *Diatessaron* of Tatian — a 'harmony' in which all four Gospels are written side by side — compiled in the second century, in Syriac.

Then there are almost 2,000 ancient lectionaries (lists of Bible passages set out for reading at different times through the Christian year). In addition, ancient writers frequently quoted from the Bible in their own books, and these quotations can also be valuable witnesses to the Bible text. The Apostolic Fathers, for instance, writing between AD90 and 160, quote from virtually every book of the New Testament. And the work of Origen gives a unique insight into ancient texts. He was a third century church leader and one of the first Bible commentators.

Which books are in the Bible?

With so much ancient evidence available to us, no sane person would deny that the Bible in our hands today is in all essential respects the Bible as it was originally written. But there is a further question. *Codex Sinaiticus*, the great manuscript found by Tischendorf, includes two writings not found in today's Bibles: the *Epistle of Barnabas* and the *Shepherd of Hermas*. *Codex Alexandrinus*, one of the other more significant ancient manuscripts, also includes parts of two epistles of Clement of Rome, together with sections of a book known as the *Psalms of Solomon*. In addition, we know that the early Greek translation of the Hebrew Bible (the *Septuagint*) also contained some 'extra' books. And the scrolls discovered by the Dead Sea include some of the same works. So which books really belong in the Bible?

This is an important question, and not even all Christians agree on the answer to it. There is no argument on what comprises the New Testament. But there are various ways of looking at the extra books sometimes attached to the Old Testament. These include *1 and 2 Esdras, Tobit, Judith, Wisdom of Solomon, Ecclesiasticus,* the *Letter of Jeremiah, Baruch, Song of the Three Young Men, Susannah, Bel and the Dragon, The Prayer of Manasseh, 1 and 2 Maccabees,* together with additional material in the books of Esther and Daniel. Christians of the Anglican tradition accept these additional works as useful for practical guidance in living, but not as an authentic part of Scripture. Roman Catholics, on the other hand, view these so-called 'deuterocanonical' books as part of the Bible itself. The Orthodox tend to follow a similar practice, though they have never made any formal decisions on the matter. Then there are the Protestant churches, which deny that these extra books — what they call the 'Apocrypha' — have any special authority at all.

Who decided which books would make it into the Bible? We should remember that this is a distinctively modern Western question. The philosophical legacy of the Enlightenment has encouraged us to want everything cut and dried, in a way that was not of great concern to people in the ancient world, nor for that matter to the vast majority of the world's people today. The search for absolute 'logical' consistency is essentially a Western preoccupation.

In the early days of the church, no one ever stopped to think about an issue like this. They had many more interesting and urgent things to do. From the very start the followers of Jesus gave a special authority to the Old Testament. The sayings of Jesus himself were soon given a special place too.

But at the outset there was no idea of a limited list — or 'canon' — of such teachings. We can see this from the way the New Testament itself occasionally refers to sayings of Jesus that are not now contained in any of the four Gospels, for instance in Acts chapter 20 verse 35. Indeed, the fact that there are four Gospels, and not one, also suggests there was no great desire to achieve uniformity through a fixed collection of the teaching of Jesus. John mentions many other sayings of Jesus not included in that Gospel, without any suggestion that what was left out was in any way inferior to what was included. It was just that it was not relevant for John's immediate purpose.

As the leaders of the church — people such as Peter and Paul — gave advice and guidance to their converts, it was natural that their words and writings should also be highly respected. They themselves seem to have felt that a special authority attached to what they wrote (see for example Galatians chapter 1 verses 7 to 9). And by the time some of the latest books were written, some of the earlier New Testament documents were already regarded as 'scripture'. In the next generation of leaders, we find the Apostolic

Fathers (people such as Ignatius, Clement of Rome and Polycarp) take a similar line. They refer in their own writings to most of the New Testament books, and clearly had a high regard for them. But they also used and valued other Jewish and Christian writings.

Perhaps the church could have lived like this for a long time, had it not been for one specific event. In about AD150 a man called Marcion left the church at Rome and announced that he had found a new message. This message, he alleged, was not actually new but had been given in secret by Jesus to his twelve disciples. They had not preserved it adequately and so its secret was subsequently entrusted to Paul. To back up this claim, Marcion made a list of those books that allegedly provided 'proof'. This selective list included only one 'Gospel' (identical with none of the four New Testament Gospels, but not too different from Luke), together with ten letters of Paul. At about the same time, there was a proliferation of other sectarian groups, all of which compiled their own lists of sacred books. In the nature of things, the books they each included were those that best served to uphold their own distinctive ideas.

In the face of arguments like this, what could the leaders of the mainstream church do in order to present what they knew to be the authentic Christian message? Since everyone else seemed to be trying to prove their case by reference to lists of sacred texts, that was an obvious place to begin. The sectarians were saying, in effect, 'Here are the books which prove our claims: what proof have you got for your position?'

By the end of the second century Irenaeus, bishop of Lyons in France, had compiled such a list himself. He also set out guidelines for deciding on the relative value of the various Christian books that were then in circulation. Those of most value, he argued, must be the ones that had a clear connection with the apostles themselves, for they had been the close associates of Jesus. In the years that followed, this principle was refined more precisely so that in the third century the historian Eusebius could list three different categories of Christian writings.

He mentions those that were certainly authoritative (the four Gospels, Acts, the letters of Paul, 1 Peter, 1 John and Revelation); those that were certainly not (*Acts of Paul, Shepherd of Hermas, Apocalypse of Peter, Epistle of Barnabas, Didache, Gospel according to the Hebrews*); and those whose status was disputed

(James, Jude, 2 Peter, 2 and 3 John). Eventually in the fourth century we find comprehensive lists of authoritative books, one from Athanasius in the Eastern section of the church (AD367), and the other from the Council of Carthage in the Western church (AD397). The books they list are the twenty-seven books of the New Testament as we know it.

These books did not suddenly become important overnight. They had already been widely used and highly regarded for centuries. The decisions made in the fourth century were simply the formal acceptance of a state of affairs that had existed for many years. It is sometimes claimed that the church leaders were trying to suppress beliefs that they themselves disliked — things such as reincarnation, or evidence for cosmic consciousness or ETIs in the Bible. But that is the exact opposite of what actually happened. The fact is that what appeared in lists of acceptable books was based on the consensus of what the overwhelming majority of Christians believed and practised. It was only because of this that the 'canon' ('rule of faith') was universally accepted. If a small but powerful group had been trying to manipulate everyone else for their own ends, we can be certain that history would have recorded it.

What about the Old Testament then? Here too there seem to be some ragged edges around the list of authoritative books. The Old Testament is a more complex collection of writings than the New. It was compiled over a far longer period — something like 1,000 years, as opposed to the sixty to seventy years of the New. And during that long period of time, cultural and social norms changed many times. Writing itself was widespread in the world of the Old Testament. Long before the age of Moses, people of a similar cultural background to the Hebrews were literate, and as long ago as 1800BC to be a scribe was a recognized profession. The earliest mention of secretaries and writers in Israel was in the days of King David in the tenth century BC, so there must have been a sizeable body of national literature in existence by then. The Old Testament makes passing references to some books of that time which have now disappeared: *The History of the Kings of Israel, The History of the Kings of Judah, The Book of Jashar, The Book of the Lord's Battles*. Even in these early days, some books were treated with special reverence.

The great prophets of Israel usually prefaced their messages with the words 'Thus says the Lord'. They believed that through them God was directly addressing his people. Moreover, they reminded the nation that this was not some new idea, for God had previously addressed them in the words of the Law delivered on Mt Sinai at the very outset of Israel's national life. Presumably this Law had not been accorded any great status, otherwise the prophets would not have castigated their people for failing to take it seriously. But by the end of the seventh century BC things were gradually changing. And by the second century BC, Jewish writers were claiming that the Law revealed to Moses had existed before the creation of the world — indeed, that it would last unaltered for all eternity.

In the meantime, other books had been given a special place, not least those associated with the prophets themselves, together with works which were of particular relevance to the life and worship of Israel — books such as Psalms, Job, Proverbs, and others.

The gradual nature of this process reflects the fact that the Old Testament is the national archive of a people, subject to expansions and additions over many centuries. If life in Israel had continued unchanged, perhaps no one would have thought of asking which books should go into the nation's sacred scriptures. But new factors soon presented this question with a particular urgency.

In 586BC, the Babylonian emperor Nebuchadnezzar destroyed Jerusalem and its temple, and removed most of the city's leading inhabitants. To be sure, the temple was restored within less than a hundred years. But from that point onwards, the Jewish people were scattered all over the known world. By the time of Jesus, Jerusalem had far fewer Jews than places such as Alexandria in Egypt or Rome. These people never lost sight of their national heritage. But without immediate access to the temple in Jerusalem it was inevitable that they should look for new ways to express their faith. Animal sacrifice had always been central to the life of the temple. Now expatriate Jews met for a different sort of worship in local synagogues. There, prayer and the reading of their national literature took pride of place. But which texts would be most useful for such a purpose? The copying and study of ancient books soon became a full-time job for many religious leaders. Immediately after the return from exile in Babylon, a similar need had arisen in Palestine itself in the time of Ezra and Nehemiah in the fifth century BC. Faced with the task of restoring the faith of their ancestors, they too had needed to identify the authentic record of that faith, so it could be handed on to new generations.

But there was a further complication. For the Jewish communities outside Palestine used the everyday language of their own towns and cities, which was Greek. Virtually none of them understood Hebrew any more, so they needed a Greek translation of their sacred books. This task was undertaken spontaneously all over the Mediterranean world. But it was the Jews of Alexandria in Egypt who took it most seriously. The translation they produced is often referred to nowadays as 'the *Septuagint*'. But this *Septuagint* was not simply a Greek Old Testament. It was not one single volume at all — for the simple reason that no one then knew how to bind writing materials together in large enough quantities to contain such a large body of literature as the Old Testament. To possess a Greek — or Hebrew — Old Testament involved a lot more than owning just a single volume. It is this simple fact that provides a crucial key to understanding which books were a part of the Old Testament.

Each Bible book was written on a separate roll of material, and a complete Old Testament required a large number of them. On top of that, many different people were busy making their own translations of the Old Testament into Greek. If you wanted to have your own copy, you needed to gather together a considerable number of separate rolls, and also decide which translation to choose from. When the Christians eventually produced a single-volume Greek Old Testament, this is exactly what they did: they made a random selection from the various translations that were in general use. And when they did so, they generally included some of the books that we now call 'deuterocanonical' or 'apocryphal'.

How did this happen? An ancient library was not like a modern one. The rolls could not be kept on a shelf. Instead they were stored in boxes, and a library consisted of a pile of these boxes. The boxes were made in a standard size and served as a sort of classification system. But rolls came in different sizes, depending on what was written on them. After the main scroll had been stored in a particular box there would often be space left — a space which might be filled with another scroll on a similar subject.

Remember too that actual writing material was of great value in the ancient world. It was not cheap, especially if it was made from animal skins. Scribes never wasted space, and blanks at the end of a roll would be filled up with other material that seemed generally related to the main subject matter. It is simple facts like these which explain why the exact contents of the Greek Old Testament seem, from our perspective, to have been so variable. But in fact the contents of the Old Testament were not as arbitrary as we might imagine.

It was another historical crisis back in Jerusalem that led to the final resolution of this state of affairs. Following the destruction of Jerusalem by the Romans in AD70, temple worship there came to an end once and for all. From now on, all Jews would have to relate to God primarily through prayer and reading their sacred books. In addition, the rise of Christianity was beginning to threaten Judaism. The disciples of Jesus were claiming that his teachings were also a part — indeed the most important part — of God's communication with his people. It therefore became a matter of urgency for the rabbis to clarify the contents of their scriptures.

As with the Christian leaders a couple of centuries later, they had a long-standing consensus to help them decide. Meeting in council at Jamnia in about AD90, the rabbis formally decided to recognize the books of the Hebrew Bible, as used in Palestine itself, as of special authority. They were fewer in number than the books circulating in Greek, partly because Greek-speaking Christians had understandably tended to regard anything written in Hebrew as of special importance. And the books of the Hebrew Bible were those that are now contained in our Old Testament.

So why do some Christians include the extra books in their Old Testament? This again has a simple historical explanation. Very few Christians ever spoke or wrote Hebrew, and their Old Testament was usually the Greek translation. They had a complete Greek Bible — both Testaments. When they produced translations into other languages, their obvious starting-point was Greek. One of the most influential of the ancient translations was the Latin version of Jerome, produced in the fourth century. He actually based much of his work on the Hebrew Bible, in consultation with some Jewish rabbis he knew. He knew that the Hebrew Bible contained fewer books than the

Greek versions which most Christians used, but nevertheless he included the extra books because of their familiarity. His Latin Vulgate became the Bible of the Western church, and through this formed the scriptural canon of the Roman Catholic church. At the time of the Protestant Reformation in the fifteenth century, the Reformers reverted to the Hebrew canon which, in their view, was more authoritative.

What about mistakes?

We cannot leave this subject without also considering the implications of the fact that all these ancient texts were copied out by hand, long before the invention of printing. It must be obvious that mistakes would be made from time to time. And there is quite a catalogue of errors that could — and did — creep in.

A scribe might just misread the text and copy it down wrongly. Or miss out a letter, a word, or even a line or two. Or write the same letter twice. Or confuse similar endings or beginnings of words. If the text was being read out aloud, then a copyist might easily mishear what was said.

Ancient texts often used abbreviations for words that occur frequently, such as 'God' or 'Christ'. If the copyist misunderstood these — or operated with a different system of abbreviations — then mistakes would easily be made. Added to all that, ancient readers (like their modern counterparts) often made notes in the margin. An inattentive scribe could easily incorporate such comments into the text itself. There is some evidence that this is what happened with the word 'Selah' which appears in many of the psalms of the Old Testament. This word was a musical direction to the temple choir and orchestra, telling them to reach a crescendo at these points. But an unmusical scribe, working from a copy with such annotations in the margin, incorporated them into the main body of the text without realizing what he was doing.

Geographical and climatic factors also affected the preservation and integrity of ancient manuscripts. A document might be stored where mice could nibble at the edges. Or pages could go mouldy and some of the writing be lost. Some think this is what happened with the New Testament Gospel of Mark. In most of the manuscripts, this ends halfway through a sentence at chapter 16 verse 8 — a curiosity that other ancient scribes tried to put right by compiling suitable concluding paragraphs. The fact that these extra paragraphs are found only in inferior manuscripts suggests either that Mark deliberately ended on a note of high drama, or that the last page somehow got lost. And where does the story now found in John chapter 8 come from? No one doubts it is a genuine account of an incident in Jesus' life. But some manuscripts include it at John chapter 21, or even at Luke chapter 21. Did some ancient scribe perhaps get the pages mixed up?

There is also the inescapable (and regrettable) fact that unscrupulous scribes occasionally altered the text quite deliberately to suit their own ideas. This still occasionally happens today. When the Jehovah's Witnesses were looking for scriptures to back up their own point of view, they found existing translations unhelpful. So they produced their own — the *New World Translation* — which, needless to say, provides plenty of evidence for their distinctive beliefs. A thousand years ago, Hebrew scholars often changed words that had a reference to Baal, the fertility god of Canaan. They substituted the word *bosheth*, meaning shame, thereby indicating their disapproval of those who got tangled up with Canaanite worship. Fortunately for us, they usually did this by altering the vowels beneath the words, while leaving the original consonants unchanged.

That introduces us to another peculiarity of these ancient texts. Hebrew had no vowels, only consonants. In due course the rabbis made up for this lack, and in the ninth and tenth centuries AD invented a complicated system of dots and dashes which they placed under the consonants, to indicate how they thought they should be pronounced. Sometimes they used these to try to insert their own commentaries on the text — as in the example above — which means that for safety we should look only at the consonants.

This presents its own problems, of course. Think of an English sentence with no vowels: th ct n th mt. Now, what are the missing vowels? We can all see that there is more than one possibility. Could it mean, 'the cat on the mat'? Or 'the act on the mat'? Maybe 'the coat in the moat'? Or even 'the cut in the meat'? The possibilities are certainly extensive, if not endless. But if we knew that the phrase occurred in a book about animals, or a clothing catalogue, or a report of a butcher's shop, it would not be nearly as difficult to decide. And this is the case in the Old Testament. The context in which a phrase is used makes its meaning perfectly clear almost everywhere.

Many of the ancient Greek manuscripts present a similar challenge to the modern interpreter. Most of them have no divisions between words, and both ancient scribes and modern scholars have to introduce their own in order to make sense of what is being said. On occasions, a double meaning can be possible. Look at this English sentence: GODISNOWHERE. What does that say? Depending on your own starting point and personal assumptions, it can mean two diametrically opposite things! God is nowhere — or God is now here.

If we had only a handful of Bible documents, all these things could be a serious hindrance to accurate translation and understanding — though it has to be said that every other text from ancient times is afflicted with the same handicaps. But they really are of no significance at all, simply because of the sheer volume of ancient Bible texts that we have at our disposal. In those few cases where there is any variation in the manuscripts, the simple application of commonsense rules and a few well-chosen questions can resolve the matter. Questions such as: Which words give the better sense? Which reading is less likely to have been made through a copying mistake? Which reading is least likely to be due to the personal theological opinions of a scribe? And which reading is supported by the oldest and best manuscripts?

This is the kind of painstaking analysis of the evidence that all major modern Bible translations are based on, and any claim that the Bible as we know it is a hoax, a forgery, or some kind of conspiracy by the ecclesiastical establishment is simply far-fetched nonsense.

4
The Bible and History

Bible manuscripts are not the only objects that link the Bible to the ancient world. When Tischendorf set off on his trips around the Middle East, he was just one of many people at the time whose imagination was fired by the prospect of new discoveries that could open up the world of the Bible in a way never before thought possible. In this chapter we will ask how the Bible stories fit into the world of which they claim to tell. Do they have a ring of authenticity about them? Can they be related to other facts we know about their world? These are very extensive questions, and to be totally comprehensive we would need to ask them of every single Bible story, one by one. That would be unrealistic, so we will just have to be satisfied with selecting a few typical examples here. Before we do that, however, we should set our questions in context. For that, we need some idea of the work of modern archaeology — and that itself is a fascinating story.

The good old days

People seem to have a perennial fascination for times and places long since vanished. One of the characteristics of our own generation is a sentimental nostalgia for 'the good old days' — days when, supposedly, life was more straightforward, people lived more simply, and horrors such as the nuclear threat or the greenhouse effect were just a twinkle in the eye of science fiction writers. 'There is nothing new in the whole world,' wrote the author of Ecclesiastes. And as far back as we can look, men and women have always been allured by the charms — real or imaginary — of generations that have disappeared forever.

Well before the Christian era, the rulers of ancient Assyria and Babylon spent much of their time preserving and exhibiting the literary and material remains of those who had gone before them. Throughout most of the ancient Middle East, these kings were more to be feared than admired, yet even the most inhumane and ruthless emperors also found time for the gentler pursuit of historical knowledge for its own sake. Perhaps absorption in other worlds blunted the sharp reality of the rough edges they had created in their own. Whatever their reasons, we today owe an incalculable debt to these men for the way in which they collected and preserved materials that were ancient even in their day. Without their passionate devotion to the heritage of their own lands, we would know a good deal less about Middle Eastern civilizations than we now do.

The famous Royal Library discovered at Nineveh in the mid-nineteenth century is generally regarded as the collection of Ashurbanipal (669-627BC). But he was only its final benefactor. The work had actually begun a century before under Tiglath-Pileser III (744-727BC). Its contents gathered together the traditions of the area going right back to the Sumerians at the very dawn of civilization itself (fourth millennium BC). At a later date, the palace of the Babylonian king Nebuchadnezzar (605-562BC), who himself features in the Bible stories, contained a museum with statues and other relics of the past. And Nabonidus (556-539BC), the final king of Babylon, spent so much time finding and cataloguing historical relics that he eventually lost his empire.

There can be no doubt that the same fascination with the past also motivated some of the rulers of ancient Greece, though there is less direct evidence. When Alexander the Great first extended his mighty empire to cover the whole of the Mediterranean lands — and more besides — it was obvious that, although his might be the most sophisticated world power up to then, it was certainly not the first. When the remnants of his empire were once again united by the Romans, everywhere they went there were constant and very visible reminders of the greatness of the past. In Egypt, the banks of the River Nile were lined with giant pyramids that even then were very ancient. Travellers bold enough to venture east towards the opposite end of the 'Fertile Crescent' that sprawled from Egypt up through

Palestine to the Persian Gulf soon found themselves face to face with the more obvious remains of other great cultures of the past: Persia, Babylon, Assyria and Sumeria. At the sites of ancient cities such as Nineveh, buildings made to last stood as permanent monuments to the extraordinary creativity and terrifying power of their architects.

Searching for the past

Not long into the Christian era the lands of the Bible were themselves added to the places of historical pilgrimage in the ancient world. Interest in sites and monuments connected with the story of Jesus and the history of his nation can be traced back to the earliest centuries of the life of the church. Following an unsuccessful revolt against Roman rule in AD132, Jews were banned altogether from visiting Jerusalem for a considerable length of time. But once the Emperor Constantine became a Christian, fellow-believers who were rich enough to make the journey found that travel to the Holy Land was relatively easy. The emperor's mother, Helena, was an early visitor, along with notable church leaders such as Eusebius, bishop of Caesarea (AD260-340), and the anonymous 'Pilgrim of Bordeaux', who went from France to Jerusalem and back, and wrote a vivid account of his journeys on his return (about AD333-334).

Private pilgrimages by well-heeled families continued throughout the Middle Ages, encouraged and facilitated by the military excursions of Western rulers into Palestine throughout this period. Though the political ramifications of the Crusades were not always fully understood at the time, there can be no doubt that this interest in the land of Palestine helped to preserve at least some of the central sites related to the Bible story. The Church of the Nativity in Bethlehem would certainly have fallen into ruins had it not been for the constant attention of European monarchs. During the eleventh and twelfth centuries they made a heavy investment in the preservation and renovation of its structures. But even this was sometimes counter-productive, for the more magnificent a shrine it became, the more popular it was as a place of pilgrimage — and by the fifteenth century the feet of thousands of pilgrims had literally destroyed the floor!

Such affluent visitors usually came back home laden down with souvenirs that they collected along the way. Blocks of stone, carvings, an inscription or two, jewellery, ancient books all found their way into the rich houses and castles of Europe at this period. By the sixteenth century, professional explorers generally went for more exciting challenges, preferring to open up the new worlds that were being discovered in other parts of the globe rather than traversing the well-worn paths of the old world.

The European Renaissance brought a fresh awareness of the grandeur of ancient Greece and Rome, and led to renewed interest in the lands of the Bible among wealthy Europeans. To have ancient artefacts by the fireside became a status symbol in Western homes, and a steady stream of treasure hunters headed East. Many things of great value were destroyed at this period and lost for ever.

But there was also a serious interest in rediscovering the ancient world. Enlightenment Europe owed a great debt to the Greek and Roman thinkers of antiquity, and many hoped that by shedding new light on the past, they might also discover new direction for the future. Archaeology began to develop as a serious way of exploring ancient cities, and rich patrons all over the continent wanted their names to be associated with such enterprises.

Two sites in particular captured the popular imagination: Herculaneum and Pompeii. These were two Italian cities not far from Naples which had been devastated by the eruption of Mt Vesuvius in AD79. Thanks to the careful work of the new scientific archaeologists, both places slowly began to emerge from centuries of volcanic ash by the mid-1700s. Ordinary people looked with amazement as they saw beautifully preserved Roman streets and houses rise from the ground as if by magic. No less impressive were the achievements of the scholars who worked in these places. Giuseppe Fiorelli had pioneered a very sophisticated method of identifying places and objects, and in 1860 he took over the Pompeii site.

Not surprisingly, the story of modern archaeology runs hand in hand with the European imperialist expansion of the day. The French emperor, Napoleon, made a number of visits to Egypt in the eighteenth century. He did not go to investigate its past, of course. But the commanding presence of the pyramids was impossible to evade, and even hardened military men could not help wondering about the meaning and significance of these strange structures and the many inscriptions found on and around them. Especially since they were the objects of all kinds of speculation as to their true origin, and their possible role in the future of the world.

Purely by chance, an officer in the French army came across a stone inscribed in three languages: Greek, and two forms of Egyptian. A brilliant scholar by the name of Jean Francois Champollion managed to use his knowledge of Greek to break the code of the other two languages, and thereby unlocked the secrets of ancient Egyptian writing. This opened up a whole new world, and the pyramid inscriptions could now be deciphered for the first time in modern history. This, together with the new optimism and self-confidence that was sweeping through Europe at the time, gave a fresh impetus to the search for the past.

The great Enlightenment thinkers had convinced themselves that the ultimate 'truth' about the meaning of life was to be found in the processes of human thinking, as people tested and tried old ideas to see what made sense in the light of modern discoveries. It now began to look as if it would be possible to rewrite history itself. Instead of trusting the judgments and opinions of people who belonged to an unsophisticated past, we could now check the facts for ourselves to see if ancient writers and thinkers could be believed, or whether their work needed amendment in the light of more perfect understanding. Before long, diplomats and explorers were falling over one another in the scramble to discover the secrets of long-forgotten cities such as Nineveh and Babylon.

In the middle of the nineteenth century the British Museum drew up a contract with the explorer Austen Henry Layard, commissioning him — in words that could have been written yesterday — to 'obtain the largest possible number of well-preserved objects of art at the least possible outlay of time and money'. Many spectacular finds found their way to Britain as a result of this policy — statues, monuments, jewellery, and much more. But it is certain that many other valuable items perished in the process, because these explorers were mostly interested in large and impressive-looking objects that would excite public opinion, and simply discarded anything that seemed less desirable.

Once suitable items had been identified, it frequently called for considerable ingenuity to get them back to Europe. Cleopatra's Needle, which now stands by the banks of the Thames in London (and which has little connection with Cleopatra!) was so large and awkward a shape that a ship had to be specially built to contain it. During the course of its one and only voyage, the ship sank and its precious cargo — weighing all of 186 tons — was raised from the sea bed only with great difficulty and eventually put on display in London.

Other items that found their way to England at this time were clay tablets from ancient Mesopotamia, written in what is called 'cuneiform' script. This consists of marks made in slabs of wet clay with wedge, or triangular-shaped instruments. The tablets would be baked hard in the heat of the sun, and when completely solid they formed durable records which could not easily be destroyed. Once linguistic experts had succeeded in deciphering the various cuneiform texts found in the area, that gave a fresh impetus to the systematic search for the dim and distant past. By 1865 a group of British enthusiasts had set up the Palestine Exploration Fund to help pay for such investigations, and similar French, German, American and — in due course — Jewish funds were to follow.

Digging up ancient cities

At this time, archaeologists worked mainly by trial and error. Some finds were so large it was impossible to miss them. Many explorers merely helped themselves to these and left everything else. But there was a major breakthrough with the work of Heinrich Schlieman who excavated the site of ancient Troy in 1870. He was a wealthy man, and was able to finance all his own expeditions. As he was digging, he noticed that the heaps of debris he was moving represented between them the entire history of the site. Each new city had simply been built on top of the remains of the previous one, and what was just rubble foundation to the ancient builders could become for the modern archaeologist an invaluable clue to the life of one generation after another in that place.

It was an English archaeologist who ultimately used this observation to develop a completely scientific procedure for archaeological digging. He was Sir William Flinders Petrie. Born in 1853, he was not the easiest of people to get along with. After his death in 1942, his friend Leonard Woolley described him as 'Essentially a free-lance, impatient of all authority, but himself an authoritarian with a dogmatic assurance of his own rightness . . . he had little interest in others' work and small respect for others' opinions.'

Epitaphs like that could be written for many of the world's great achievers. But to be fair, Petrie had some excuse for growing up to be so self-opinionated. As a child, he lived a very isolated life and never really mixed with any other children. Consequently, he never had a chance to develop the social graces that are learned most easily in childhood play. He was said to be too delicate to go to school, and was largely self-taught, helped and encouraged by his parents. His father had an interesting and varied career as a civil engineer, chemist and surveyor, while his mother (unusually for those days) was herself a professional geologist, with quite an interest in ancient coins. By the age of sixteen, William knew the British Museum galleries as well as modern teenagers know the pop charts. His father encouraged him to develop an interest in surveying ancient earthworks around England. This was intended to be a preparation for a trip to Egypt, where Petrie senior wanted to test various magical theories about the origins of the pyramids.

In the event, young William went alone to explore the pyramids — and demonstrated that his father's speculations made no sense at all. But he also learned the importance of being precise about examining and measuring ancient objects. And he fell in love with the land of Egypt and its fascinating history. He never had much money to support his work, but he made some remarkable discoveries there. A major breakthrough came when he realized that it was possible to use pottery as a means of dating the relics from the past. This one single observation changed the whole face of excavation, and earned him the title 'father of modern archaeology'.

Excavations in the Bible lands always turn up more pottery than anything else. For every bucket of significant objects, archaeologists recover dozens of buckets of pottery. The reason is simple. Pottery was always in common use, and it was very easily broken — but it was virtually impossible to destroy completely. Moreover, similar sorts of pottery were used all over the ancient world. And fashions of size, shape, texture and decoration were constantly changing.

Some styles stayed in use over a long period of time, others lasted for only a short while. So when the same types turn up at several different locations, the chances are that the layers of material in which they are found date back to about the same time.

Petrie inspected a wide variety of pottery styles from many different places, and concluded that it would be possible to use them as a reference chart for the dating of all sorts of objects from the ancient world. He called this chart the 'Ceramic Index'. Today it has been refined so exactly that it is possible to give very precise dates to ancient objects on the basis of the sort of pottery with which they are surrounded.

Petrie himself first visited Palestine in 1891, and examined the site known as Tell el Hesi, which he (wrongly) identified with the Bible city of Lachish. He soon discovered that excavating there was quite different from working in Egypt. Instead of the large and conspicuous monuments that dot the Egyptian landscape, the typical site in Palestine is a large mound, or tell. Many of these sites look just like small hills. They can be as high as 30 or 40 metres, and are often covered with trees or grass. But under the surface they conceal the ruins of an ancient city.

Some cities were built on hills, so they would be easy to defend. But many tells actually started at ground level, and have been raised to their present height in the normal processes of building over many years. Ancient buildings were generally made of mud and wood, and when a town was destroyed by an enemy, or just fell into decay, the inhabitants would gather any available materials that could be reused, and set about building a new settlement on top of the ruins of the old. This way, the new level could be as much as 2 or 3 metres higher than the one before it. So over many years, the ground level gradually rose, and if an X-ray photograph was taken through one of these mounds, it would look like a giant cake, with many different layers superimposed one on top of another.

This is a real challenge for the excavator. To make the most sense out of it, each layer needs to be kept separate from what is above and below. They may be on the same site, but the layers are actually the remains of different cities, separated in time by hundreds of years. To mix the remains of one city with that of another would be very misleading. In theory, the best way to keep them separate would be to start at the top of the pile and slice off each layer in turn. But in practice, this is impossible. It would take a very long time, and cost too much money. So archaeologists have learned to compromise. They usually slice the mound up as if it were a giant cake. This makes it possible to see a cross-section of the mound's contents. By the 1930s, explorers were agreed that this was the way to do it, and the sites of many Bible places began to open up.

Despite such sophisticated techniques, digging up a Bible city still presents its problems. Where you dig determines what you will find. If you cut a slice at the wrong place, you might find nothing — whereas a slice only a few metres away may produce something truly spectacular. Even knowing which mounds to look at is not easy.

In 1963, a 23-year-old excavator called Paulo Matthiae decided to excavate Tell Mardikh. There are dozens of mounds like it all over Syria, and more experienced experts told him he was wasting his time. Nothing of interest would ever be discovered there. But Matthiae had a feeling that they were wrong, and for twelve years he went against all the best advice. Then in 1975, he unearthed a stunning collection of texts dating from 2300BC. That itself was surprising enough. But what really dumbfounded everyone was that his texts were in a language no one had ever seen before! He had unearthed the city of Ebla, which was the capital of a flourishing empire in central Syria back in the third millennium BC. No one had even imagined its existence, but as a result of Matthiae's determination his discovery has led to the rewriting of much of the history of the time.

The development of reliable archaeological procedures had wide-ranging repercussions for understanding the Bible. It was now possible to see the Bible's world through the eyes of people other than the Bible writers. Ever since the heady days of the Enlightenment, rationalist thinkers in the West had suspected — even if they could not prove — that the Bible was probably faulty in some way, and could not be trusted to give a reliable account of things as they really were. With new discoveries coming to light, modern people could look at the same events from the perspective of ancient Assyrians, Babylonians and others, and see who was really telling the truth! The best archaeologists denied that these were their motives: theirs was the altogether 'purer', more objective consideration of just finding out what the ancient world was like. Or so they said. In any case, they were unable to stop others taking their discoveries and using them for such propagandist purposes.

In fact, it soon proved impossible to explore the annals of ancient Assyria and Babylon without coming into direct contact with characters and events mentioned in the Bible.

Israel and the world powers

Throughout the Old Testament period, Israel lived in a very precarious position between the two superpowers of the day, in Mesopotamia and Egypt. These two, one at either end of the Fertile Crescent, were engaged in a continual struggle for power over the whole region stretching from modern Iran and the Persian Gulf westwards to the Mediterranean Sea. Israel was in the middle, and often became involved.

One of the early Egyptian finds made by Sir Flinders Petrie, in 1906, actually contained a reference to Israel. This is a large granite monument, measuring some three metres high by almost two metres wide. It was first constructed in the reign of Pharaoh Amenophis III (1406-1370BC). But on its reverse side a later pharaoh, Merneptah (1224-1214BC), had inscribed a long poem to celebrate his victories against the Libyans and others. Among the places he mentions is Canaan, and in the list of peoples conquered we find this statement: 'Israel is laid waste, his seed is not . . .' Some have tried to integrate this statement very precisely with the Bible stories of the exodus of the Israelites from Egypt, in an effort to discover the precise date when it took place. That is not really possible. But it undoubtedly shows that by about 1220BC the Egyptians knew of a nation called 'Israel' among the various kingdoms of Canaan.

Other Egyptian evidence thought to relate to the same period of Bible history is contained in the Tell-el-Amarna Letters. There are almost 400 of these documents, written in Akkadian, and dating from the early fourteenth centuryBC. They are letters written by various rulers in Canaan and Syria to Pharaoh Akhen-aten (1369-1353BC) and his predecessor Amenhotep III (1398-1361BC). After their discovery by a peasant in Middle Egypt in 1887, they soon came to the attention of Bible scholars, who were struck by the fact that they mention groups of marauding tribes who are called 'Aperru', or 'Habiru' — words which sound surprisingly similar to the Old Testament descriptions of Abraham and his descendants as

'Hebrews'. Some were tempted to jump to the conclusion that 'Habiru' and 'Hebrews' were one and the same. That is going further than the evidence allows. But many experts believe that the general upheavals reflected in the Amarna Letters may well portray the international context out of which the nation of Israel was born.

We are on much firmer ground when we move to the other end of the Fertile Crescent, especially during the heyday of the great Assyrian Empire based in northern Mesopotamia, mostly around the cities of Nineveh, Asshur and Kalah. The people of this region always had a strong and stable culture. But it was not until the days of Israelite kings such as Saul and David that they began to think of expanding their empire westwards. In doing so, they developed highly trained and super-efficient armies. They were also meticulous in record-ing all their achievements — including their many forays into Israel itself. The annals of Sennacherib (705-681BC), for example, include a description of how the Assyrian emperor attacked the kingdom of Judah in the days when Hezekiah was king. This is how the Assyrian report — preserved in cuneiform script on a large clay cylinder — tells the story:

As to Hezekiah the Jew, he did not submit to my yoke. I laid siege to forty-six of his strong cities, walled forts and to countless small villages in the vicinity and conquered them by means of well-stamped earth-ramps and battering rams brought thus near to the walls . . . Himself I made a prisoner in Jerusalem, his royal residence, like a bird in a cage. I surrounded him with earthwork in order to molest those who were leaving his city's gate . . . I reduced his country but I still increased the tribute and the presents due to me as his overlord which I imposed upon him beyond his former tribute to be delivered annually . . . Hezekiah did send me later to Nineveh . . . thirty talents of gold, eight hundred talents of silver.

The same story is told in the Bible in 2 Kings chapters 18 and 19. That account naturally tells what the siege looked like from where Hezekiah was. But the remarkable thing is that the two accounts complement one another in an extraordinarily precise way.

One Assyrian monument actually has a line drawing depicting a king of Israel mentioned in the Old Testament. This refers to the northern kingdom of Israel, with its capital in Samaria. The

Assyrians had already destroyed the kingdom some time before the episode with Hezekiah in Jerusalem. The Israelite king in question — Jehu (842-815BC) — had come to power in a ruthless coup which not only succeeded in getting rid of the entire royal family of his predecessor Ahab, but also alienated the neighbouring nations of Phoenicia and Judah. Ahab had managed to form a Palestinian coalition to keep the power of the Assyrians at arms' length. But shortly after Jehu came to power, Shalmaneser III (859-824BC) broke through with a vengeance, besieging Damascus and taking over much of Syria. To try to preserve their own independence, both Phoenicia and Israel were forced to pay him tribute.

Shalmaneser describes all this in great detail on a large black obelisk which was discovered by Sir Henry Layard at Nimrud in 1840. On it, he records that Jehu offered him 'Silver, gold, a gold beaker, golden goblets, pitchers of gold, lead, staves for the hand of the king, javelins . . . ' and pictures Jehu himself bowing down low to present these gifts. This drawing of Jehu is the only contemporary portrait we have of anyone named in the Bible. The picture itself adds nothing to our specific knowledge of Jehu. But the whole story underlines in a most graphic way the truth of what the Bible itself says — namely that Jehu and his successors were unable to do much without the constant threat of Assyrian disapproval. As he bows low to the ground before the Assyrian emperor, he is only doing what dozens of other local kings of the region did both before and after his time.

Before Jehu came to power, Ahab and his father Omri had established a powerful and stable society based on their capital city of Samaria. Samaria is an important place as it was the only major new city to be founded by Israelites. Elsewhere they just rebuilt towns and villages that had existed long before their own nation emerged. Omri and Ahab were determined to build a city of grandeur and beauty, and Samaria was well known for its magnificent buildings. Old Testament writers often refer to the ornamental ivory carvings which were its crowning glory, for example in 1 Kings chapter 22 and Amos chapter 3.

Modern excavators have discovered ample evidence of the luxury of that era. Middle Eastern royal palaces were often decorated with ivory, and Samaria has produced hundreds of intricately carved pieces. Their designs suggest that Ahab imported both the ivory and the carvers from neighbouring countries. Some pieces show signs of having been inlaid with gold and other precious metals and jewellery. All of which breathes new life into Amos' bitter words about the habits of the kings of Samaria: 'Woe to those who lie upon beds of ivory and stretch themselves upon their couches . . . '

These are just a few examples of Assyrian and Babylonian accounts relating to the land of the Bible. There are many others, and they frequently refer to the stories and personalities of the Old Testament. Quite often they provide us with additional information that helps to set the Bible accounts in a wider perspective than would otherwise be possible. Instead of having just one eyewitness account of these events, we have two or three.

Written materials such as the Assyrian and Babylonian annals are not the only way to shed new light on old stories. Sometimes the excavation of a place can help us to understand how particular Bible incidents may have taken place. Here we return to the siege of Hezekiah in Jerusalem, already mentioned from the records of the Assyrian king Sennacherib.

Hezekiah was determined to have a showdown with the Assyrians, and as part of his efforts at renewed independence he reinforced the walls of Jerusalem and built up an impressive armoury. The city was built on an enormous rock, which offered splendid security and made it virtually impregnable. But its strength was also, paradoxically, its main weakness. The main water supply was at the foot of the rock, outside the fortifications. That meant any long siege was almost certain to bring disaster for the inhabitants. Even before Jerusalem became 'the city of David', its original Jebusite inhabitants had constructed a secret internal water shaft to give them easier access to the springs. According to the Bible story, it was through this shaft that David managed to get into the city. So it obviously was not totally impregnable — though it must have been incredibly difficult to penetrate all the same. In any case, the intervening years had seen many changes in the city's size and shape, and Hezekiah now needed to construct a new tunnel. The Bible tells how Hezekiah 'built a reservoir and dug a tunnel to bring water into the city': he 'blocked the outlet for the Spring of Gihon and channelled the water to flow through a tunnel to a point inside the walls of Jerusalem'. This information is found in 2 Kings chapter 20, and 2 Chronicles chapter 32.

As long ago as the Middle Ages, pilgrims to Jerusalem had known there was some connection between the Pool of Siloam — at the south-east corner of the old city — and the Spring of Gihon beyond the walls. But exactly where it ran remained a mystery until 1880. Two young Arab boys were swimming in the Pool of Siloam when one of them found himself in a small passage leading out from the sheer rock face. Further investigation revealed that a narrow tunnel had been cut through the solid limestone rock. It was only just large enough for an adult to squeeze through with difficulty. For over 500 metres, the passage winds upwards carrying water from the Spring of Gihon, outside the city walls, to the Pool of Siloam which was presumably well inside them.

But there was more. Just a few yards from the Siloam entrance, there was an inscription scratched on the tunnel walls, written in Hebrew. It tells how the tunnel was constructed in the space of about six to nine months, and graphically describes the excitement of workers digging through from each direction, as they could hear the scraping and hammering of those on the other side — and eventually broke through to meet in the middle. Considering that they were digging in an S shape and through solid rock, and with no magnetic instruments to find the direction, this was a remarkable achievement. They must have had considerable stamina too, for they worked in almost total blackness and with very little air. Workmen clearing rubble from the tunnel in 1910 found they could work only for very short periods before they needed to come up again.

Sennacherib did come and, in his own words, 'shut up Hezekiah like a bird in a cage'. He created havoc elsewhere in the land, but he never broke through the defences of Jerusalem. Thanks to the rebuilt walls and their new water supply, its inhabitants were able to resist quite a long siege by a sophisticated and determined opponent. And due to a chance discovery we can today visualize their achievement more graphically than ever.

Romans and Christians

Archaeology has a more extensive and direct bearing on the stories of the Old Testament than of the New. Israel was a nation, interacting with other nations, so we can expect its rulers and history to be referred to in other sources. By contrast, the New Testament reflects the life and beliefs of a small minority group scattered around the various towns and cities of the Roman Empire. The first Christians were mostly insignificant people. No one erected statues in their honour nor — in the first century at least — did any of them rise to positions of eminence in the Roman hierarchy. So it is less likely that we would find other references to events in their churches. But there are a handful of discoveries that shed light on the life of these earliest Christians.

Paul of Tarsus was a Roman citizen, and he moved freely through much of the Mediterranean world, frequently meeting Roman officials and politicians. It would be unrealistic to expect official Roman documents to mention these meetings: Paul was simply not important enough for that. But at least we should be able to expect that if he worked in the mainstream of the empire, his life story would make sense in that context.

The Bible contains two sources of information about Paul. The Acts of the Apostles is a general account of the beginnings of the church, though most of it is about Paul. But Paul was a prolific writer himself, and more than half of the New Testament consists of letters he sent to his friends. He never intended these letters to tell the story of his life, but they naturally contain many snippets of information about him. Both Acts and Paul's letters make reference to specific places and people. They generally date these incidents by reference to one another, rather than relating them to any of the great events taking place in the Roman history of the time. Paul dates the events after his conversion by reference to various visits he made to Jerusalem. He mentions theses in Galatians chapters 1 and 2. But we have no certain dates for any of these. The book of Acts mentions various Jewish festivals in relation to Paul's travels — but again, it is a matter of careful guesswork to piece them all together into a coherent set of dates.

One place that features prominently in Paul's work is the Greek city of Corinth. It had a long history, but was rebuilt as a Roman colony in 46BC, and in Paul's day it was a prosperous trading centre. It has been extensively excavated, and modern visitors can walk around its streets and soak up a little of the atmosphere that Paul himself must have known. Of course Paul was not a tourist, and often found himself on the receiving end of violence and prejudice against the message that he proclaimed. On one occasion the Jewish community in Corinth brought him before the local Roman governor, claiming that 'This man is trying to persuade people to worship God in a way that is against the law'. These words are found in Acts chapter 18. The remains of the Jewish synagogue where these arguments took place can still be seen, and the governor's court was held at an imposing rostrum of white and blue marble that stands in the very centre of the town.

Acts names the governor as Gallio, the elder brother of the famous Roman philosopher Seneca. An inscription found at Delphi indicates that he was proconsul of Achaia for the year AD51-52. Acts also mentions that in Corinth Paul met with Aquila and Priscilla, who had fled to the city as a result of the Emperor Claudius' expulsion of Jews from Rome — which was in AD49. Putting this information together with the further fact that Paul had been in the city for eighteen months before he met Gallio, it has been possible to piece together the chronology of Paul's life, and to see that the Bible's stories about him authentically reflect circumstances in the world of his day.

The culture of Canaan

Many historical finds relate directly to Bible passages. They demonstrate overwhelmingly that the Bible stories faithfully reflect the times and places in which they took place. Sometimes — as with the Assyrian inscriptions — we can confirm specifically the details of particular events. Occasionally, information from the wider world can be combined with details in the Bible to give a more comprehensive picture of places and people. But more often, archaeological finds will give insights into the life and thought of a particular place, and so help to illustrate and bring the Bible stories to life for us.

One such find was made at Ras Shamra, near the Syrian seaport of Latakia just opposite Cyprus. Nowadays it is a popular tourist resort, with a restaurant at the site and a fully equipped resort hotel just down the road alongside another important excavation at Ras Ibn Hani. Early in 1928, a local farmer by the name of Mahmoud Mella az-Zir was ploughing a field overlooking the sea when he discovered a large flat stone. Carefully prising it loose, he soon realized it covered the entrance to an ancient tomb. He quietly removed a few items and took them to a local antique dealer. But it was inevitable that news of his discovery would leak out. This area was ruled by the French at the time, and they kept a staff of professional archaeologists there for the sole purpose of checking out such finds. According to local legends, the mound of Ras Shamra had once been the site of a great city, and at the deserted bay where Mahmoud Mella az-Zir lived a prosperous harbour had existed.

Local officials immediately recognized that this site would repay closer attention, and within a year a professional archaeologist had arrived from Strasbourg. His name was Claude F.A. Schaeffer. He began work in March 1929 not far from the shore at the bay of Minet el-Beida. This was some distance away from the large mound, but he soon realized he was on to something big. Purely by accident, he had started digging in the middle of an ancient cemetery, and important objects soon came to light. He could have spent many weeks here. But his curiosity got the better of him and he soon switched his attention to the remains at Ras Shamra just a short distance away. When he started on the mound itself, there was very little to be seen, apart from a great crop of fennel (the Arabic name simply means 'Head of Fennel'). It was certainly not easy to decide where to start digging. So he began at the highest point, which looked as if it might contain the remains of ancient walls. Besides, some locals claimed to have found valuable objects there.

Schaeffer soon knew he had chosen the right place. In no time at all, he was unearthing scores of fascinating objects, as well as the remains of intriguing buildings. Among the finds were vast numbers of clay tablets inscribed with cuneiform writing. This was not surprising in itself, for by the 1930s hundreds of them had been unearthed all over the Middle East. But the writing on these was quite different from anything he had seen before. Other texts used hundreds of symbols to record their messages.

These seemed to be using an alphabet with not more than about twenty or thirty letters. Charles Virolleaud was the director of the Antiquities Service of Syria and Lebanon, and a gifted linguist. He was fascinated by these strange texts, and in a remarkably short time he began to grasp what they were saying. He shared his findings with other scholars working in Europe, and by the end of 1930 they had cracked the code of this remarkable new language.

By now, Schaeffer was really excited about his discoveries, and in early 1930 he made his way back to the site. This time he had more back-up resources, including thirty French soldiers to guard both the site and the experts. Safety could not be taken for granted, as just the previous year another French archaeologist had been murdered by robbers in the same area. Once more he started with the cemetery area, looking over what he had found the year before and also identifying a large building with many rooms, which turned out to be part of a tomb for the kings of the nearby city. But the mound held an inexorable fascination for him, especially the area where the tablets were unearthed. By digging a deep pit right through the mound, Schaeffer established that people had lived here as far back as the third millennium BC. But still more tablets kept turning up — and in several languages, using different types of writing. The scribes of this ancient city were exceedingly well educated. The diversity of languages here would be comparable to a modern person being equally at home in English, Arabic, Chinese, and Russian! Many other valuable objects were also discovered, and a picture of life in this ancient city was gradually pieced together.

But what was its name? The American scholar W.F. Albright wondered if it might be Ugarit, a city mentioned in other sources but so far undiscovered. This intuition was soon confirmed as Virolleaud found the name Ugarit in many of the texts. Here was a new city and a new language — Ugaritic — which would have a far-reaching impact on our knowledge of the Bible.

Work came to a standstill in 1939, with the outbreak of World War II. Schaeffer went into the French Navy. After the war he returned and stayed there right through until 1969. The excavations of Ras Shamra are among the most extensive of any town or city related to the Bible. And after more than half a century of work, we know a great deal about the life of ancient Ugarit. The most prosperous time for this city was from about 1500 to 1200BC, and this is the age about which we are best informed. Thanks to this remarkable discovery, we can imagine what it was like to live here in a culture long since past — ruled by kings with strange-sounding names like Niqmadu, Ibiranu, Ammistamru, and others of their family.

The city was actually the capital of a small kingdom, with about 200 villages scattered over an area of 1,300 square miles. Most of the people were farmers. But with three seaports there must have been a fishing industry as well. Rich traders from Ugarit certainly owned fleets of ships, and to judge from the size of some of their anchors they must have been large vessels up to 30 metres long and weighing more than 200 tons. Timber was also an important product, along with cloth and various metal objects — domestic implements as well as gold and silver jewellery. These were all sold in world markets, transported by sea under the protection of a large Ugaritic navy. The city had many large and impressive houses, some of which contain the remains of substantial libraries. It was a community with great wealth. But the documents discovered here also show a community with a strong sense of social responsibility.

The king took a personal interest in the welfare of his citizens, showing special concern for widows and orphans and other marginalized people. Religion was important as well. Apart from the royal palace, the temples of Dagan and Baal were the largest buildings, and their large staff played an important part in the life of the nation.

Surprisingly, it all seems to have disappeared almost literally overnight towards the end of the thirteenth century BC. At this time, the powerful 'Sea Peoples' were advancing eastwards across the Mediterranean Sea and conquering most of what stood in their way. They must have been very powerful, for they feature in many texts of the period. The Philistines, who play a big part in the Old Testament story, were a part of this invading force. Ugarit had survived invasions before (notably by the Hittites in about 1360BC). But they were not strong enough for this new assault, and the city and its inhabitants were simply wiped out not long after 1200BC. The end came so swiftly that the ovens in the royal palace still contained the remains of cuneiform tablets that were in the process of being baked hard.

The story of this kingdom, its kings and its people, is a fascinating tale by any standards. But for Bible readers the most important things from Ugarit are its texts — something like 1,400 of them, written in a language very closely related to the Hebrew language in which the Old Testament was written. Some tell the story of the gods and goddesses who were worshipped in Ugarit. But these deities were not unique to this one city, and their names were already familiar from other parts of Palestine, Syria and Egypt. Some of them appear in the Old Testament itself, including one of the leading characters, Baal. Six tablets discovered in 1930-31 give a lot of basic information about this god, though none of them tell us just how he was worshipped. Many gods and goddesses appear in these stories. There is El, the chief of the gods, and his female companion Asherah. But Baal, the weather god, is undoubtedly the most important, along with his lover Anat, the goddess of love and war. One story tells how Baal was attacked by Mut, the god of barrenness and sterility. As in many ancient fertility myths, he overcomes Baal and his powers of life and virility, and scatters his body to the four corners of the earth. While El, the father-god, leads the heavenly mourning for his lost son, Anat, the goddess of fertility, goes out to take her revenge:

She seizes Mut, the son of El, with the knife she cuts him, with the shovel she winnows him, with fire she burns him, with millstones she grinds him, on the field she throws him. The birds eat his remains, the feathered ones make an end to what is left over.

Even that does not secure the total annihilation of Mut, who comes back to life again and fights face-to-face with Baal himself — a conflict resolved only by the intervention of El, who banishes Mut so that Baal may once more reign. Baal's power is brought back as he renews his sexual relationship with Anat — and that in turn ensures the fertility of the earth and its inhabitants for another season.

These themes are familiar from fertility religions throughout the world. They were of particular importance in Canaan. Agriculture was the mainstay of life, and without the rains that fall from October to April nothing would grow. When the rains stopped in May, it seemed as if Baal was dead and needed to be revived. Some experts believe the story of Baal's revival by Anat was the central feature of an annual New Year festival in ancient Canaan. On this occasion, held every autumn, the king and a female temple official would act out the story of Baal and Anat, to make sure that all would be well for another year. Certainly there is plenty of evidence for sexual intercourse featuring prominently in Canaanite religion, and to engage in this at the right time and place was as much a part of the job of a farmer as the actual operations of agriculture.

Evidence from places such as Ugarit have given a fascinating insight into the world of the Bible. It may not convey the same sense of excitement as when we find the names of Bible characters actually spoken of by other nations. But it is the most valuable kind of archaeological evidence of all. Because of what we know from Ugarit, we have a far clearer idea what it must have been like to live in ancient Israel. The hopes, fears, challenges and possibilities facing ordinary people come vividly to light in the remains of this unique Canaanite city-state. We can say without hesitation that the picture presented by the Old Testament writers is a perfectly authentic reflexion of what it was actually like to live in Canaan. Although that in itself does not prove the truth of their message, it does give them a degree of credibility that requires us to take them seriously.

False trails

Time was when it looked as if archaeology might well solve all the outstanding questions about the Bible. But life is rarely so simple. Especially here. True, our understanding of the Bible's world is light years ahead of the received wisdom of a hundred years ago. Looking back to some of the theories propounded in the nineteenth century by the 'experts' of the day, it is hard to believe that they could come up with such far-fetched notions as some of them did. Our knowledge of the simple facts of Bible life has been immeasurably enlarged by the painstaking work of generations of committed explorers.

But archaeology is not all plain sailing. Months of diligent work can lead to very meagre conclusions. And the assured results of one age have sometimes had to be jettisoned in the light of new information. This is the way any scientific discipline works: mapping out theories, and then testing them by the evidence. Everything we have looked at so far in this chapter falls into the category of findings that have been checked and double-checked by so many diligent researchers that their credibility is not in doubt. But it would be wrong to give the impression that everything has been that simple. The fact is that excavations at some Bible sites have been disappointing in the extreme.

The city of Jericho is a particularly striking example. Probably the oldest city in the world, continuously inhabited since about 9000BC, Jericho and its dramatic conquest by Joshua occupies a central position in the story of how Israel came to be established as a nation in its own land. Historically, Canaan was never politically united before this. It was ruled by a whole series of independent city-states — like the one at Ugarit. Jericho was one of the largest. It was rich and well fortified, and the story told in Joshua chapter 6, climaxing in the apparently miraculous collapse of its walls, is one of the highlights of the entire Old Testament.

The site of ancient Jericho — Tell es Sultan — was one of the first mounds to be excavated in Palestine. Ernst Sellin and Carl Watzinger visited it for the first time between 1907 and 1911. At that time, the significance of using pottery as a key to dating was not yet fully understood. These early explorers were mainly interested in finding and removing large objects for their wealthy patrons rather than setting the whole city in its context. But they did uncover some walls. Two walls, in fact, made of sun-dried bricks, about 8 to 10 metres high and constructed in a concentric ring separated by a gap of about 4 metres between them.

The outer wall was 2 metres thick, and the inner one was twice that. Heavily influenced by the rationalist historians of their day, these two scholars had actually been rather sceptical about the Bible story when they first went to Jericho. But as a result of what they saw, they concluded that the outer wall had been destroyed about 1200BC, and therefore must be actual wall which fell before Joshua's armies.

This judgment led to intense interest in the site of Jericho. But it was 1930 before another major expedition started digging there. This time it was led by the English archaeologist John Garstang. After six years' hard work, he uncovered other sections of the city walls, and discovered that the space between the two walls was full of rubble — the remains of houses built on top of them. He also found the whole site was littered with piles of ashes and charred wood. There had evidently been a great fire in Jericho at the same time as its walls had collapsed. As near as Garstang could tell, it had all happened about 1400BC — though others were still convinced by Sellin and Watzinger who had dated the destruction a bit later. But in the light of what was under the ash, the date hardly seemed worth quibbling about. Garstang had no doubt that the discovery of walls that collapsed in such a great inferno within the period 1400 to 1200BC could mean only one thing: he had found the walls destroyed by Joshua. The Bible story was true, after all!

When Garstang came to write an article for the London *Times* of 6 December 1933, he had no hesitation in calling it 'The story of Jericho. Fable and evidence'. He was quite sure that 'definite conclusions' were now possible, and he said so in his opening paragraph. This is how he described what he had found:

The evidence from all sources is thus in complete agreement that the normal life of Bronze Age Jericho ceased abruptly about 1400BC, during the reign of Pharaoh Amenhotep III. As to the nature of the end, all the buildings of the Palace area and the few houses against the city wall bear witness to a catastrophe attended by an intense fire while the rooms were in active occupation. Earlier observations, supplemented by deeper excavations made this year, show that the city walls fell, shaken by earthquake, in the same age, and the signs of conflagration are plainly visible upon and amidst their ruins. It is reasonable to infer that walls and buildings perished at one and the same time through the same cause or causes.

Though he thought an earthquake was involved, he found no difficulty integrating that with the Bible story. Did not the Old Testament itself say that just a short time before the final assault on the city, a rock fall had blocked the River Jordan and allowed the invading Israelites to cross over on dry land? The fact, recorded in Joshua chapter 6, that 'the priests blew the trumpets . . . they gave a loud shout, and the walls collapsed . . . Then they set fire to the city and burnt it to the ground, along with everything in it . . . ' seemed to match his findings perfectly. Garstang had no doubt that he had discovered the city destroyed by Joshua, and that it happened just as he Bible said.

He was not the only one to think like this. Sir Charles Marston, one of Garstang's collaborators back in England, wrote excitedly about the royal tombs of Jericho. He considered that the ramifications of this surprising discovery went far wider than just the Joshua story. Writing in the London *Times* on 26 January 1932, he made the following claims:

One tomb is dated as of the joint reign of Hatasu and Thotmes III, and this is of exceptional interest in confirming the modern theory that the Exodus must have taken place after the death of Thotmes III.

Hatasu was the most masterful princess in Egyptian history, and during the reign of Thotmes II, which lasted for 13 years, she ruled the whole of the country. It is extremely probable that it was she who discovered the baby Moses among the bulrushes.

The Bible dates coincide. Under the protection of Hatasu, Moses became an important official at Court, and a favourite of the princess.

After the accession of Thotmes III, Hatasu continued to exert wide authority in Egypt and incurred the bitter hatred of the new king. On her death in the fourteenth year of his reign, he seized all her possessions, and her favourites — including Moses — were compelled to flee the country. Thotmes III reigned for about 53 years and, as recorded in the Bible, Moses spent 40 years in exile. Not until after the death of the king did Moses return to Egypt, and then the Exodus took place.

These claims generated great excitement back in the thirties. One of the most extraordinary of all Bible stories had finally been proved to be true! This euphoria lasted for a long time. Indeed, Garstang's results are still occasionally quoted as authoritative even today. But the fact is that he was completely and utterly mistaken.

Garstang was a good archaeologist, and knew well enough the importance of dating his finds by reference to the layer of the mound at Jericho in which he found them. That was how he arrived at his startling conclusions. What he did not know, however, was that at the very point where he was digging, the top of the mound had been worn away with the passage of time. Several layers had disappeared altogether — and for that reason, the remains he found were actually from a much lower (and older) level than they appeared to be. In fact, they were from a city that had flourished on the site a full thousand years earlier than any possible date for Joshua. More recent excavations have revealed that virtually nothing now remains of the city that he attacked. Certainly nothing like enough to reach any reliable conclusions about the nature of the Bible story. So although we now know that Jericho is the oldest city on earth, we know next to nothing of its life at the time when Israel was emerging as a nation. Unless other finds come to light — which seems unlikely — archaeology simply cannot help us to understand this most intriguing of Bible stories.

The Bible in its world

Archaeologists are constantly shedding new light on the Bible. We now know a good deal more about the two Bible languages, Hebrew and Greek, than any previous generation thanks to the discovery of other texts in these and related languages. Poetic symbolism in many parts of the Old Testament can now be seen for what it is in the light of the finds at Ras Shamra and elsewhere. The decoding of the great Assyrian, Babylonian, and Egyptian records has given us unique insights into the sort of pressures facing the kings of Israel and Judah, and lets us understand why the prophets of the Old Testament felt as they did about the political and religious cross-currents of their day. In relation to the New Testament, new evidence has shown us what crucifixion meant in the Roman world.

Sites visited by Paul and other early Christians have yielded treasures that help us to appreciate the magnitude of their missionary task. And what does it all prove? Quite simply, it shows beyond any doubt that all these books accurately reflect the world of which they purport to speak. The Bible is not a forgery, written many centuries after the events it describes. Of course, it reflects a particular viewpoint on these events — that of ancient Israel and Judah, and then the disciples of Jesus. Just as the records of other people reflect their own national perspectives. But it is that very fact that gives us greater confidence in dealing with the Bible stories.

History is not really a problem for the Bible — nor for the modern reader. The real questions start to come in thick and fast when we look at the details of the stories. For the Bible's perspective includes a world where anything can happen. This is no ordinary story. As well as the leading lights of the day, God features in it too. And he seems to engineer some pretty remarkable things. There is a supernatural dimension to it all, not usually found in history books — certainly not those written by Western Enlightenment thinkers. What can we make of all this? How does it fit in with our modern mind-set? How much can we believe without being irrational? And especially, what can we believe about Jesus, the Bible's central figure? These are deep waters. Largely uncharted too. But that is where we must head in the next couple of chapters, if we are to do justice to this remarkable book — as well as to our own intelligence.

5

Discovering God

The Old Testament was originally written in Hebrew, the traditional language of the nation whose story it contains. By the time of Jesus, it was widely available in Greek. That was the everyday language used throughout the Roman world, and the Greek Old Testament was avidly read by Jewish communities all over the empire. When Tischendorf discovered the massive *Codex Sinaiticus*, its Old Testament sections contained this Greek translation — the *Septuagint*. We have already considered its composition and contents in a previous chapter. But where did it come from?

Origins of the Bible

An ancient story sets out to answer that most intriguing of questions. Called *The Letter of Aristeas*, it contains the reminiscences of a court official of that name who served in Egypt during the reign of the Greek pharaoh Ptolemy II Philadelphus (285-247BC). Following the sudden death of Alexander the Great in 323BC, his empire was divided among his generals. Ptolemy was the name of the soldier who inherited Egypt, and his family ruled the country until the Romans came on the scene.

Alexander had a great passion for the Greek way of life. He was determined that in all the lands he conquered his new subjects would speak, think, and act in the best traditions of Greek culture. He was convinced that this was the only way in which the world could ever be fully civilized. It was a bold — and remarkably successful — move. So successful that this unified culture based on all things Greek — 'Hellenism' as it came to be known — lasted for almost 1,000 years. His successors shared this vision. And since Palestine was a part of his empire, Greek civilization soon made an impact there too.

From about 320BC until 198BC, southern Palestine was under the control of the Greek rulers of Egypt. On the whole, they tolerated the religious scruples of the Jewish people. But they forced many Jews to emigrate to the city of Alexandria, which at the time was underpopulated. Many more went voluntarily, and there was soon a thriving Jewish community in this new Egyptian city. Naturally, for a city named after Alexander, its language was Greek. It was inevitable that sooner or later the Hebrew scriptures would need to be translated into this everyday language so that future generations of Jews could have easy access to the traditional faith of their nation.

Unlike some of his predecessors, Ptolemy Philadelphus was a peaceful man who loved culture. He was determined that his land would become a great storehouse for all the wisdom of the ancient world. He already had a head start, with all the monuments left behind by previous generations of Egyptian monarchs. So he put much of his own energy into the establishment of a great library. He scoured the world looking for books to include in his collection, and soon amassed almost a quarter of a million volumes. Though he cannot possibly have read them all, he still wanted more. Naturally, all the classics of Greek literature were there. But his collection was cosmopolitan and international in scope. He and his librarian, Demetrius, began to search for other suitable literature wherever it might be found. With such a large Jewish element in the population, it was only a matter of time before their attention focused on the Hebrew Bible. Such a large body of literature certainly deserved to be given a place in the royal library. But first it would need to be translated into Greek.

The king sent for the leaders of the Jewish community in Alexandria, to ask their advice. They were highly flattered that anyone should take such an interest in their religion, and readily agreed to co-operate. It was decided that a letter would be sent to the high priest in Jerusalem, asking for his help in supplying copies of the sacred text along with trustworthy scholars who would undertake the work of translation. Aristeas took the letter, accompanied by another Egyptian courtier by the name of Andreas. To ensure that they were well received Philadelphus ordered the release of more than 100,000 Jewish slaves in Egypt, and sent to Jerusalem 100 talents of silver as well as many sacrifices.

Eleazer, the Jewish high priest, responded favourably. He appointed seventy-two men for the task, six from each of the twelve tribes. All had impeccable moral and religious credentials, as well as being experts in both Hebrew and Greek. They made the journey back to Egypt, taking with them the precious scrolls on which the scriptures of their nation were inscribed in golden letters.

On their arrival, they were warmly received by Philadelphus himself, who duly acknowledged the value of their scrolls by bowing down before them seven times. He spent a full week feasting and asking questions of the Jewish scholars — one for each of them every evening — before they were finally packed off to the Island of Pharos to begin their work. According to one version of the story, each translator was shut up in a separate room, so that they all worked independently of each other. There they stayed for precisely seventy-two days. When the time was up, the seventy-two scholars emerged from their seventy-two rooms, and to everyone's amazement their seventy-two translations were word-for-word identical! The Jewish people in Egypt were naturally delighted. But so was Philadelphus. When the translation was read out to him, he at once recognized it must be divinely inspired:

When the whole work was read to the king, he was greatly astonished at the spirit of the lawgiver. And he said to Demetrius, 'How is it that none of the [Greek] historians or poets ever thought of mentioning such great achievements?' He replied, 'Because the Law is holy and has been given by God — and some of those who did think to mention it were smitten by God and desisted from the attempt.' He said that he had heard Theopompus tell how when he was too rashly intending to introduce into his history some of the incidents from the Law which had previously been translated, his mind was deranged for more than thirty days '. . . I have been informed too,' he added, 'by Theodectes, the tragic poet, that when he was intending to introduce into one of his plays something recorded in the Book, he was afflicted with cataract of the eyes; and, suspecting that this was the reason for his mishap, he besought God's mercy and after many days recovered his sight.'

Philadelphus must have wondered whatever he had done when he heard these encouraging tales. Which explains why he played safe himself: 'he made obeisance, and ordered that great care should be taken of the books, and that they should be guarded with proper awe.' With that, he gave the new translation pride of place in his library, and sent the translators back to Jerusalem with extravagant rewards.

Not everyone believed that sort of story, even in the ancient world. But it reflects the way that many people would like to think about the Bible. If it is in some way 'inspired', they reason, then surely it must have fallen from the skies, as it were — complete and perfect, just waiting to be read. Writing about the *Septuagint* translators, the Jewish writer Philo, a near-contemporary of Jesus, commented:

With none present save the elements of nature, earth, water, air, heaven . . . they became as it were possessed, and, under inspiration, wrote, not each several scribe something different, but the same word for word, as though dictated to each by an invisible prompter . . .

There is no shortage of religious books that claim to have been written in this way. Including several modern ones. On the night of 21 September 1823 a young farm-hand by the name of Joseph Smith had a vision in his room in Ontario County, New York. In it, he believed he came face to face with an angel from God by the name of Moroni. This angel brought a message:

He said there was a book deposited, written upon gold plates, giving an account of the former inhabitants of this continent, and the source from whence they sprang. He also said that the fulness of the everlasting Gospel was contained in it, as delivered by the Saviour to the ancient inhabitants; also that there were two stones in silver bows — and these stones, fastened to a breastplate, constituted what is called the Urim and the Thummim — deposited with the plates . . . and that God had prepared them for the purpose of translating the book . . .

Three years later, on 22 September 1827, Smith went to the appointed place on the hill Cumorah, unearthed the magic stones, and with their help translated the golden plates into English. The angelic messenger returned to take them away again immediately the job was done, but Smith's work was published in 1830 as *The Book of Mormon* and is still the sacred scripture of the religious sect of that name. In his own day, Joseph Smith was widely disbelieved. Not least because he and his friends became involved in many scandals that shocked ordinary people — and certainly led them to doubt that he could possibly, as he claimed, have had a face-to-face meeting with Almighty God and Christ himself!

But religious devotees today still make similar pretensions. The various channelled revelations that are so popular among searchers for the 'New Age' all claim to be direct communications between some other world and our own. It is easy to see why such works should be so appealing to a culture which seems unable to handle the kind of world it has created. For books like this claim to have the power to deliver their followers from the harsh realities of everyday existence, and put them into direct contact with another, less threatening world. All we need do is to read them, for what they say is the exact and specific message that some divine or extra-terrestrial being wishes us to hear. To be fully understood, they need neither interpretation nor further elaboration.

No doubt God could have sent the Bible down ready-made, as it were. It might have saved a lot of hassle had he done so. But the fact is that he chose a different procedure. The Bible does not consist of the actual words that God spoke through some ancient channeller. Nor was it dictated from heaven to the individuals whose names are now found in its various sections. Amos, Jeremiah, Isaiah, Luke, Paul, John — and the rest — were all real people. They wrote their books, usually on their own initiative, because they wanted to share their own experience of God with others of their own time and place. This may seem to be a very haphazard way to produce an authoritative religious text. But as the Canadian sociologist Marshall McLuhan observed, 'The medium is the message.' The way the Bible came into existence is a crucial part of what it has to say.

Behind all modern channelled revelations lies the assumption that life in this world is not as important as we think it is. Some claim it is all an illusion, others that it is simply irrelevant. Either way, spiritual reality and true personal fulfilment is to be found in some other dimension of existence. As long ago as the second century AD, Gnostic groups on the fringe of the Christian church were making similar claims. They believed that the real meaning of life could only be found by escaping from this world into some other, more spiritual sphere of existence. Over the years, some Christians have also acted as if they believed life here is only a preparation for the real thing up in heaven.

But that is not the message of the Bible. From first to last — Old Testament as well as New — it shows a God who is prepared to affirm our existence here in this world. The place where we live and work day by day is part of his world — and he is as deeply committed to it as we are. The Bible does not deny the essential goodness of human existence, nor does it suggest we need to escape from the world in order to find God. The opposite, in fact, for throughout its pages the Bible stories relate how God has actually come into our world in order to share it with us. For me as a spiritual pilgrim, that is very good news. It means that God is interested in my personal concerns — and as I look for meaning and personal transformation, he offers it to me here and now. He reassures me that, however the system seems to treat me, I am important to him. And I have a part to play in creating a better society in which I and all the world's people can find true fulfilment and spiritual meaning.

The Bible and its message holds the key to this way of living. It does not contain esoteric and mysterious spiritual messages. It tells in simple words how ordinary people have discovered God in everyday things — and found their lives transformed. This is the Bible's great strength as a source of spiritual wisdom. But it is also a potential weakness. The fact that it refers to specific times and places and people means that if I am to get the most out of it for my own spiritual search, I need to handle it with care, and with due regard to the sort of book it is, and for the concerns of its many human authors.

What is the Bible?

If you want a Bible today, you go along to the bookshop and buy one. It looks and feels like any other book. A fairly long one, admittedly — and often printed on thin paper so that its extensive contents can be bound as a single volume. But as soon as you open its pages, it is obvious that it is not quite what it seems. For a start, the primary division of its contents is not into chapters, but into 'books' — and then, within those books we find chapters, which in turn are sub-divided into 'verses'. Over and above that are the two obvious major divisions of the whole work into 'Old Testament' and 'New Testament'.

In addition, if you know any Christians who regularly use the Bible as a source for information or inspiration about their faith, you soon discover that to make sense of it, you do not apparently have to begin at page 1 and read right through to the end. When I first became interested in the Bible, I found it very puzzling that all the Christians I knew seemed to imagine there was actually something wrong with doing that. The Bible seemed to make most sense to them if read in only small sections of no more than a dozen lines at a time. I eventually learned that this is not the only way to read it. But the very fact that most of its readers would not dream of proceeding through from start to finish at least alerts us to the fact that even at this very basic level the Bible is no ordinary book.

The fact is, of course, that the Bible is not just one book at all. It is actually an anthology. A collection of sixty-six different books, each one with its own writer, and its own subject-matter. What is more, these sixty-six books were composed in very diverse times and places. The earliest sections of the Old Testament were written a thousand years before the beginning of the Christian era, whereas the latest bits of the New Testament were composed towards the end of the first century AD. Most writers find their work takes longer than they expect. But a book that takes a thousand years to write? That has got to be something else. The Bible's contents actually seem to reflect an even longer period of time. Its earliest dateable stories take place in the Stone Age, and the latest occurred in the sophisticated world of the Roman Empire. And in between is an exceedingly diverse collection of literature.

To describe it as an anthology is to do it less than justice. The Bible is several anthologies. The Old Testament is the national archive of the Jewish people. It begins with the story of their first ancestor Abraham, and reflects the varied moods and changing circumstances of national life through to the middle of the second century BC. The various books of the Old Testament are typical of what we would expect to find in the archives of any nation. Some tell the story of the people Israel and their great heroes.

Others reflect the poetic and musical traditions of the developing community. Yet others contain collections of political and religious messages relevant to different times and situations. Then there are snippets of drama and fiction, as well as other books that do not fall easily into any of our modern categories.

If we took these books along to a library, it is unlikely that the librarian would place them all on the same shelf! And what is true of the Old Testament is also the case when we move on to the New. This time we find not a national archive, but a somewhat random collection of documents relating to the life of the earliest Christian communities. They are the sort of raw material which any modern historian would be happy to deal with. Stories of the founder of the Christian church stand alongside accounts of the exploits of the first followers of Jesus — together with ordinary everyday letters written by church leaders to encourage and help new Christians. Here too there are some bits which are hard to classify at all — books such as Hebrews or Revelation. Like the Old Testament, the books of the New document the story of a specific group of people. But they are not just history books. There are many things we would like to know that they do not tell us. To construct a comprehensive history of either Israel or the early church requires the skilful and imaginative use of the materials contained in the Bible, together with other information relating to the world in which it all took place.

How was the Bible written?

Nowadays a busy author can sit down with a word processor or blank sheets of paper, and write a book. A schedule can be drawn up so that the right amount of time can be allocated to the job. The author can log her progress as she works, showing exactly when the work was started, and recording the precise instant at which it was completed. When the work is completed, electronic wizardry can count the number of words and compile a comprehensive index. But national archives are not written that way, even in the twentieth century. They evolve much more slowly and in a more diffuse way over many years. They frequently take centuries, and they are never the work of just one person. The history of a nation — or of a group like the earliest church — will always be the product of many people, not all of whom are remembered by name. At particular stages — especially in times of national crisis — the story may be edited and brought up to date by being applied to new circumstances. And ultimately, it will settle into what becomes its final, normative form.

We can see this process at work in many parts of the Bible. In chapter 3 we looked at the way the books of Samuel and Kings often quote from other ancient sources which provided the information on which their finished account was based. Like modern historians, the writers of these books utilized materials from a variety of sources and wove them together to give a coherent view of the history of their people and its meaning. The writers of the Gospels in the New Testament did the same. Both Luke and John state quite openly that they gathered together the reminiscences and recollections of other people about Jesus — often in written form — then read them all through, and wrote their own stories on the basis of what they had read. In both these cases, later authors took the traditional stories of their group and used them to present a fresh and distinctive account of their subject-matter — whether the history of Israel, or the story of Jesus. What is more, they were obviously writing to apply it all to the needs and questions of their own contemporaries. The sort of information they included therefore often reflects the debates of generations much later than the time of the original stories they were using.

Understanding the Bible is not the same as reading a modern book — nor even a classic of ancient literature written by a single author such as Julius Caesar, Tacitus, or Thucydides. To appreciate it correctly, we need to look at each Bible book separately, and try to understand it within its own terms of reference. We can assess history books by reference to the historical procedures of the day — and, as we have seen in a previous chapter, the findings of archaeologists and other researchers can be of help here. Poetry is quite different. Its 'truth' is not a matter of factual statements, but of the aesthetic appeal of its imagery and the extent to which it authentically reflects real life. Books of fiction can also communicate important truths about the nature of human experience, and here again their lasting quality can be judged by how true to life they are.

What is the Bible about?

In spite of the fact that the Bible consists of many different pieces of literature, it nevertheless contains just one essential story. It has many heroes — from Abraham and Moses through to Jesus and Paul. But all their stories converge on just one subject: God. He is the one character who features on all its pages, and whose story gives unity and coherence in the midst of so much obvious diversity and difference.

The Bible's main story-line begins midway through the book of Genesis, with Abraham and his wife Sarah. A childless couple living in ancient Mesopotamia, they have a remarkable spiritual experience in which their lives take on a new direction, as they migrate west and south to begin a new life.

The land of their birth was no stranger to the religious quest. Ur, their original home, was the site of an impressive temple-tower built in the third millennium BC, that still reaches up to the sky even today. Its precise function is still a bit of a mystery. But it was probably related in some way to astrology. The ancient inhabitants of this region spent much time trying to use the stars and the planets to discover the meaning of their own lives. In this respect, Abraham and Sarah would not feel out of place in the modern world. Things such as planetary positions, events in dreams and the pattern of tea-leaves were all a part of the regular equipment of earnest searchers for truth. No doubt Abraham and Sarah had dabbled in all this, searching for the meaning of life in the signs of the zodiac and other esoteric places.

And then it happened. Exactly what, and how, the Bible does not spell out in detail. But when God stepped in and spoke to them, they knew it was the real thing. They packed their bags and went off into the sunset, with only the promise of God to guide and inspire them. A strange promise it was too. For it spoke of them becoming the parents of a great nation — when in reality they were not parents at all. But as the story unfolds, they have a son, Isaac, and eventually their family is so large they are almost a nation. At any rate, there are enough of them for it to be worthwhile for the pharaoh of Egypt to use them as a major source of slave labour for his building projects.

By now, a little time had passed — perhaps as much as 400 or 500 years. There is a good deal of debate as to who this pharaoh actually was. Tradition identifies him with Rameses

II (1290-1224BC). He certainly had many impressive building projects, including the reconstruction of the ancient city of Tanis as his own capital — a project mentioned in Exodus chapter 1. In any event, the Old Testament story is more concerned with the promises of God than the threats of Pharaoh. And by now, the promise first made to Abraham — that his family would become a great nation — was looking decidedly shaky.

Until somebody else had a remarkable and life-changing experience. This time it was Moses. Brought up among the ruling classes of Egypt, but actually born into a Hebrew family, Moses was living in obscurity with a family of wandering shepherds in the Arabian desert. One day while watching his sheep, his attention was attracted to a bush that was on fire. Nothing odd about that, under the hot desert sun. But this one seemed as if it was never going to burn out. So Moses went to investigate. Only to discover himself being addressed by the same God who had so unexpectedly burst into the life of Abraham and Sarah a few centuries before. The story is told in Exodus chapter 3. This time the message was, if anything, even more dramatic. Though the slaves in Egypt had little time for anything but the daily grind of work, food, and sleep, God had not forgotten his promise. He had given his word that Abraham's family would be a free nation. And so they would. Moses was duly commissioned to take a few initiatives, and in due course they were slaves no longer.

It was important for these people to understand how and why they had so unexpectedly escaped from slavery. It was certainly not their own achievement: none of them had even thought it possible. Nor was it because of the brilliant strategies of Moses. It was because of the love of the God of Abraham, which these many years later still extended to the members of his family. At least that is what Moses told them, as they camped around the foot of Mt Sinai following their escape from Egypt. Here they came into personal contact with this remarkable God. Listened to his repeated promises. Received his laws. And undertook faithfully to serve him as a mark of gratitude for all he had done for them.

Eventually, it all came true. They got their land. They even grew into a significant power under their kings David and Solomon, a thousand years before the birth of Jesus. But not without a struggle. These were challenging times, as they came to terms with their great spiritual heritage and tried to work out its meaning in the changing circumstances of life in Palestine. Abraham had been a wandering shepherd. So too had Moses. And the events at Sinai all took place in the desert. This God who made such great promises seemed to make sense in that sort of context. But what did he know about growing crops?

That was the key question for people who were now farmers. Some of them played safe. Though David had come to power trusting in the God of Abraham and Moses, and Solomon had built a magnificent temple in his honour in Jerusalem, still it seemed only prudent not to write off altogether the old gods and goddesses of Canaan. Worshipping the God of Moses — Yahweh — along with native deities like Baal would give a two-way insurance. As time went on, a majority of ordinary people began to think this way. Especially after their kingdom was torn in two by civil war following the death of Solomon, to become two nations: Israel, based on Samaria, and Judah with its capital in Jerusalem.

Both kingdoms were reasonably prosperous — particularly Israel. But the kings of both states frequently cut corners where religion was concerned. It was often politically expedient to compromise, by worshipping the gods of the superpowers — especially Assyria — alongside the God of their own nation. More sensitive thinkers were puzzled by this. Considering that the nation would never have existed at all had it not been for God's loving initiatives, how could they even contemplate forsaking the God of their forebears? This was the message of the prophets — a long line of radical religious teachers, beginning with Elijah in the ninth century BC, and extending over the next 400 years and more. Addressing the citizens of the northern kingdom of Israel in the eighth century BC, Hosea made one of the most impassioned and moving appeals in any literature, found in chapter 11 of his book:

*The Lord says, 'When Israel was a child, I loved him and called
him out of Egypt as my son. But the more I called to him, the more
he turned away from me. My people sacrificed to Baal; they
burnt incense to idols. Yet I was the one who taught Israel to walk.
I took my people up in my arms, but they did not acknowledge
that I took care of them. I drew them to me with affection and
love. I picked them up and held them to my cheek; I bent down to*

them and fed them ... How can I give you up, Israel? How can I abandon you? Could I ever destroy you? ... My heart will not let me do it! ... For I am God and not man ... '

For the prophets, religious faith did not exist in a separate compartment from other aspects of life. They were not concerned merely with theology. The nature of their beliefs about God also determined the social priorities that their nation should have. At the heart of the Old Testament faith was the demand that God's people should base their actions on the behaviour of God himself. His character had been demonstrated supremely in the escape from Egypt — the exodus. He saw that things were bad there, and stepped in to change the situation. This is why the ideal Old Testament society always had a special place for the dispossessed, the oppressed and the disadvantaged. The prophets reminded their people that under God's laws all women and men must be equal. They had all started out as equals — they were all slaves. That meant that economic and social exploitation of one class by another was not only deplorable — it was a fundamental denial of the very heart of the nation's faith.

This cut right across the natural assumptions of most people of the time. In other nations, the king had rights and privileges just because he was the king. Other religions guaranteed those privileges — which was perhaps one reason why so many rulers of Israel and Judah were anxious to embrace them. But the Bible's God was different. Elijah was not slow to tell King Ahab that he was in the wrong when he was thinking of the compulsory purchase of the vineyard of his neighbour Naboth in order to extend the royal gardens. His queen, Jezebel, did the obvious thing and had Naboth put to death. But Ahab himself was not so sure, for he recognized that such behaviour was contrary to the will of God. Other prophets put across the same message. Even the dutiful performance of religious rites could be no substitute for fair and honest behaviour. Micah says in chapter 6 of his book:

What shall I bring to the Lord, the God of heaven, when I come to worship him? Shall I bring the best calves to burn as offerings to him? Will the Lord be pleased if I bring him thousands of sheep or endless streams of olive oil? Shall I offer him my first-born child to pay for my sins? No, the Lord has told us what is good. What he requires of us is this: to do what is just, to show constant love, and to live in humble fellowship with our God.

This was a demanding faith indeed. And one which ultimately the people were unable to keep. It was a good deal easier to perform ceremonies in temples than to go out and love their neighbour. More comforting to convince themselves that God's love made them special, rather than to share that love with other nations — as Abraham had originally been instructed to do. And all too easy to invoke the name of God to justify some of the most barbarous and inhumane actions under the guise of national security.

Ahab's son, Joram, was the last of his family to occupy the throne in Samaria. He was displaced in a fierce and violent coup by an army officer called Jehu — the same Jehu whose picture appears on the Black Obelisk of the Assyrian king Shalmaneser. Jehu came to power in a blood-bath which annihilated not only the royal family of Israel, but also their royal relatives from Judah as well. While Jehu enjoyed a meal in the captured stronghold of Jezreel, he amused himself by watching the palace dogs tear the body of Queen Jezebel limb from limb. And this bloodthirsty performance had been inspired by an unnamed 'prophet' claiming to speak in the name of God!

The inconsistency of a so-called God of love apparently issuing messages like this does not escape the notice of most modern readers of the Bible. But it was not ignored at the time either. Two or three generations later, the prophet Hosea denounced this behaviour. He declared in words found in Hosea chapter 1 that God had been misrepresented and that Jehu's family would reap the inevitable moral consequences:

The Lord said to Hosea, '. . . it will not be long before I punish
the king of Israel for the murders that his ancestor Jehu committed
at Jezreel. I am going to put an end to Jehu's dynasty. And
in the Valley of Jezreel I will at that time destroy Israel's military
power.'

About the same time, Amos also denounced flagrant violations of human rights, in Israel and Judah as well as other nations. It was too easy to use religion as a cover for selfish greed and militaristic imperialism. The twentieth century has witnessed plenty of both — often perpetrated by Bible-reading nations.

Perhaps that is one reason why the Old Testament contains so many stories of mistaken brutality, inspired by a false view of God's nature. Jesus made it categorically obvious that such behaviour is contrary to God's will. But we should not forget that the basic story-line of the Old Testament teaches the same lesson. It was only a matter of time before the moral fibre of the nation descended from Abraham had been eroded to such an extent that first Israel, and then Judah, collapsed and disintegrated. By 586BC it looked as if it was all over. The Babylonian Nebuchadnezzar had smashed the walls of Jerusalem and removed its leading citizens. As they languished in exile, there seemed little hope for the future. Until God stepped in once again. First by reviving national hopes through the teaching of some remarkable prophets, and then by enabling those who wished to return to their homeland to do so under the leadership of Nehemiah and Ezra.

But it was never to be the same again. By the time of Jesus' birth, searchers after spiritual truth were looking for something new to happen, in which the original promise to Abraham could finally come true — the promise that God would bring blessing into the lives of all nations. And of course it did. In the life, death and resurrection of Jesus, and through the gift of the Holy Spirit given to his followers, God demonstrated once again that, despite much misunderstanding of his will, his love for the world and its people was undiminished. Jesus announced the arrival of God's new kingdom — and displayed its presence in his own remarkable deeds. Deeds which were continued through the disciples and succeeding generations of Christian believers. No one can doubt that the message of the New Testament is based on God's love, freely shared with all humanity through these pivotal events of human history.

It is sometimes argued that this was a fundamental departure from the story of the Old Testament. As if a God of darkness and judgment had been replaced by a God of loving care. But this is at best an over-simplification, at worst a plain untruth. Ideas like this were popularized in the early twentieth century mostly by Protestant theologians sympathetic to the Nazi cause in Hitler's Germany. But they are offensive to the Jewish people, and misrepresent the essential core of the Bible's message. Human nature being what it is, God was sometimes misunderstood and misrepresented — and the Bible bears witness to that fact. But from start to finish, the Bible's God is motivated only by his own love for the world and its people.

Danger — God at work

So far so good. But of course there is more to the Bible's story than that. A lot more. Other characters make their appearance from time to time, and there are many sub-plots that develop alongside the main thread of the narrative. But what makes it all truly unique is that God keeps stepping in. Most history is a matter of cause and effect. Like baking a cake, the ingredients you put in determine the product that you end up with. And the way the ingredients are mixed affects the quality of the cake. If the cake turns out to be a disaster, then close analysis of ingredients and method will tell you why.

The Bible, however, is not like that. It is the unpredictable and the extraordinary that determine the shape of its story. There was no logical reason why the slaves should have escaped from Egypt. But God stepped in and turned things upside down. And he does that repeatedly throughout the history of Israel and the life of Jesus and his followers. Jesus not only declares his message in words: he puts it across in remarkable deeds as well. As well as talking about 'the bread of life', he also feeds hungry people. As well as offering new light to the spiritually blind, he also gives sight to the physically blind.

Two hundred years ago, even Christians viewed all this as a definite weakness in the Bible's message. When rationalist historians, inspired by the great achievements of the Enlightenment, began turning their attention to the Bible many Christians were filled with dismay. They knew there could only be one outcome: the Bible's simple acceptance of the existence of the supernatural and the miraculous would be ridiculed and discredited by sophisticated thinkers. As a result, theologians began to deny that the essence of the Bible was to be found in these things. Instead, they claimed, the core of its message was to be identified with more nebulous concepts such as human experience, and the way people felt about God. This had the desired effect of removing the Bible from the realm of serious scientific investigation. For science only deals with facts, not opinions. But it also weakened considerably the Bible's own insistence that God is not a personification of my own feelings and spiritual searching, but is a transcendent all-powerful personal being who can and does interact with this world.

In those days, most scientists took a very mechanistic view of how things work. The law of cause and effect ruled supreme, and the existence of absolutely fixed and unchangeable 'laws of nature' was everywhere taken for granted. Nowadays, we know things are nothing like so simple. The majority of the world's people have always been open to belief that there is a spiritual dimension to existence, as well as the physical world we see all around us. Western thinkers who are gradually breaking out of the imperialism that has marred their culture for the last 200 or 300 years, find it more and more difficult to dismiss this as a 'primitive' set of ideas. The intellectual imperialism that assumed only Western philosophers could have an accurate perception of the truth has been weighed and found wanting. So has the historical imperialism of last century, which worked on the assumption that people as ancient as the writers of the Bible must, by definition, have been unsophisticated and gullible.

It is no longer possible to dismiss belief in the supernatural as the sole preserve of naive cranks and half-wits. As we saw in our introductory chapter, it is now very firmly back on the agenda of a majority of serious thinkers in the West. Surprisingly, perhaps, this is partly due to the work of twentieth-century scientists. Especially Albert Einstein, whose theory of relativity first promulgated in 1905 — together with the quantum theory of Max Planck — has changed the parameters of all discussions about what scientific consistency might mean. To put it simply, the laws of nature so confidently described by Sir Isaac Newton and other Enlightenment scientists are nothing like as fixed and predictable as we once thought they were.

Some have used these new insights to argue that the universe as we experience it is actually an illusion, and the only form of objective reality is personal consciousness, which in turn is a part of some mystical entity that is also present in the physical world of plants and animals. As a result, many of the leaders in modern scientific investigation are also mystics who see the future of our world intimately bound up with personal self-awareness and integration with cosmic forces and primal cosmic entities. The discovery of black holes and quasars by astronomers and space explorers has only served to back up such speculation. For whatever such phenomena eventually turn out to mean, it is clear that within them the 'normal' rules of space and time do not operate.

One of the clearest lessons of the last 200 years is that it is unhelpful, and usually misleading, to make religious belief depend on current scientific theories. But in terms of how we understand the world and its workings, there is no doubt that belief in miracles and the supernatural can no longer be said to be incompatible with scientific theory. That does not mean that every alleged miracle should be accepted uncritically. But it does mean we can examine the evidence put forward for a particular occurrence, and assess it on its merits rather than dismissing the supernatural as simply 'unbelievable' or 'impossible'.

In point of fact, many people find the most amazing things supremely believable nowadays. The alleged sighting of UFOs all over the world, combined with a growing awareness of psychic forces such as ESP, and the mysteries of things like out-of-the-body experiences, has led many to a heightened sense of spiritual expectancy. Some of these claims should be treated with a good deal of careful scepticism.

Erich von Daniken is one of the best-selling novelists of the twentieth century, with his many books in which he claims that the meaning of life is all related to visits to our planet by extra-terrestrials. Indeed, he has even claimed that we are all descended from them, and that the human race as we know it originated somewhere between 10,000 and 40,000 years ago with the arrival of super-intelligent astronauts from outer space, who mated with the humanoids who then inhabited the earth, to produce a new species, homo sapiens. Later, these extra-terrestrials returned to teach basic skills such as building, engineering, writing, and navigation. How else, he asked, can we explain the construction of the pyramids? Or the intriguing ruins of ancient Inca civilization, perched precariously on the peaks of the Andes? Or, for that matter, the exodus, or the insights of the Old Testament prophets, or indeed, the work of Jesus?

These extraordinary claims have provoked much discussion. It all sounds convincing, because von Daniken produces highly detailed descriptions of 'evidence' to back it up. But experts have found much of these detailed allegations to be completely unfounded. For example, he claims that the culture of the Sumerians in ancient Mesopotamia must have been inspired by extra-terrestrial intelligences because it appeared, miraculously as it were, among semi-savages not long before the time of Abraham. However, we know for certain that it did not happen like that. Far from appearing instantaneously, Sumerian culture was a long time in the making, and its detailed development can be traced over a period of something like 6,000 years, between 9000BC and 3000BC. Plenty of time for it to have grown naturally out of the increasing maturity and sophistication of those responsible for it.

Again, he claims that the massive pyramid of Cheops could not have been constructed by native Egyptians without some outside help — and that when its height is multiplied by a billion, it equals the distance from earth to the sun, thus suggesting some cosmic connection. But this calculation is simply wrong: the height of the pyramid bears no relationship to the distance to the sun, not even when multiplied by a billion! In any case, we have a good idea how the pyramids were constructed. Remains of ropes and ramps and various specialized tools have all been found, suggesting that the building levels were fixed relative to the surface of the River Nile. Moreover, when von Daniken describes these ancient extra-terrestrials, they turn out to look remarkably similar to modern astronauts — and their space vehicles need launching pads and runways just like modern airplanes. This looks suspiciously like the kind of historical imperialism we have already noticed — the assumption that, on the one hand, ancient people were mostly primitive savages, but if there were one or two super-brains among them, they must have looked and thought just like modern Westerners!

The Bible does not discourage serious searchers who are looking for the meaning of life and the cosmos. But it does not leave us to our own unaided devices in discovering answers. The questions that we ask today are as old as time itself. They were certainly all addressed by people back in Bible times. What is life about? Where can I find personal meaning, fulfilment, and transformation? And how can I know that I have found the right answers? Answers that are reliable enough for me to stake my entire life on?

The central conviction of the Bible is that these answers can all be found in Jesus. Ever since the life of this remarkable person, millions of his followers have been convinced that they are in touch with the real power behind the cosmos through their simple trust in Jesus as God's Son, their commitment of their lives to his care, and their experience of his supernatural presence through the Holy Spirit. Whether they are right, we shall have to decide for ourselves. But no serious spiritual pilgrim can ignore Jesus. Which is why we must now head in his direction.

6

Jesus at the Centre

A small boy was chatting with an adult in church one Sunday. 'I don't think I'll be here next week,' he said. 'In fact, I don't really like church much at all.'

'I'm sorry to hear that,' replied the adult — who rather enjoyed the security of the regular weekly ritual. 'What do you dislike most of all?'

'Well, it's the songs you sing.'

'Yes, I suppose they can be a bit boring sometimes.'

'Oh, it's not that,' said the bright-eyed child. 'They're all full of bad language.'

'Bad language?'

'Yes. Words like God Almighty and Jesus Christ.'

Believe it or not, that is a true story. Thousands of people in the West today know absolutely nothing whatever about Jesus. He might as well be a visitor from another planet. Some think he was.

But even a superficial knowledge of Jesus provokes an immediate reaction. He is a controversial figure by any standards, and holds a compelling fascination for all who come in contact with him. He has frequently been despised. The Romans put him on a cross, and even his own people rejected his teachings. For others he is a source of personal inspiration and practical guidance. He has been the subject of all the world's greatest artists, and the merest glimpse of this mysterious person has the power to stir the emotions of the toughest of people.

The Kelvingrove Art Gallery in Glasgow, Scotland, contains one of the most daring pictures of Jesus ever painted. Entitled 'Christ of St John of the Cross', it is one of the great masterpieces created by the twentieth-century Spanish surrealist Salvador Dali. It shows Jesus on the cross, lifted high above the whole universe, while below three fishermen go about their daily work. Writing in 1952, the artist said this: 'My aesthetic ambition in this picture . . . was that my Christ would be beautiful, as the God that He is.' A steady stream of visitors go to Glasgow from all over the world just to see this remarkable image. Its position at the end of a long dark corridor only serves to heighten its impact for those who come to gaze and wonder. For the artist used a medium that gives it a translucent, almost other-worldly sparkle. It conveys a powerful yet simple message: this figure is at the centre of the whole cosmos.

Jesus gives meaning to the way the world is made, opening a pathway of light through which the deep secrets of the universe can be revealed, and imparting new significance to the things we all do day by day. The second-century Clement of Alexandria had not seen Dali's painting, but he expressed the same reality when he wrote: 'The Lord has turned all our sunsets into sunrise.'

Artists and mystics are not the only ones to have been moved to greatness by the contemplation of the life and teachings of this man Jesus. He has been acclaimed as a hero — a prophet, even — by more than one of the world's great religions. The Quran commends him as a person with unique insights into the nature of God. Mahatma Gandhi, the founder of modern India, first came across the teachings of Jesus when he was a young man studying in Britain, and in later life he based much of his philosophy of 'non-resistance' on what he read in the Sermon on the Mount. Modern devotees of the *Course in Miracles* believe that much of it is a revelation channelled from Jesus himself to address key concerns of our own day. And millions of ordinary people all over the world study his words carefully, hoping to discover there the secrets of successful living.

But who was Jesus? What can we believe about him? Was he just a good man? Or was he God? Perhaps he was both? How important is he? What relevance, if any, does his teaching have to life in today's world? And where is the real Jesus to be found? There is plenty of room here for different opinions about the answers to these and other similar questions. But whatever we do with Jesus, we cannot ignore him and be true to our own personal search for the ultimate meaning of it all.

Jesus of Nazareth

The story of Jesus' life is deceptively simple. A wandering teacher spends something like three years of his early adult life drifting around rural Palestine. And 2,000 years later, we are still talking about him. More than that: we date our calendar from the year of his birth, and he has had a decisive significance for the whole course of world civilization. Some teacher. Some message.

But in his own context, Jesus' lifestyle and appearance was not all that remarkable. Palestine played host to many itinerant religious teachers at this time. Politically, the Romans were firmly in control of things, and every street corner held a visible reminder of their presence. As Jewish people went about their daily business, they had to accommodate this sinister occupying force that had taken over their land. More than that, they had to face up to the fact that if, as they believed, they were in some special way 'God's people', then that was difficult to square with their present circumstances. Their whole way of life was under serious threat.

The Romans demanded absolute loyalty from those they conquered, and as a way of getting what they wanted they insisted on putting down indigenous cultures and replacing them with the allegedly superior way of life of Greece and Rome. The Mediterranean world was to find unity through the imposition of a single culture. Everyone would speak Greek, observe Roman customs, pay Roman taxes, and do as the emperor demanded. Even worship him as a god, if that was what he decreed.

A crisis like that would bring any nation to a political crossroads. But for Israel, there was more at stake. Historically, their culture had been an expression of their faith. There was no way they could adopt Roman and Greek ways of thought and action without rejecting their own age-old beliefs. It was not possible to acknowledge the emperor as a divine being and still believe in only one God. To accept Roman sovereignty conflicted with a deeply-held conviction that God was their true king. The arrival of the Romans heralded more than just political confrontation: it meant spiritual and moral disintegration as well.

As far back as anyone could remember, the Jewish people had always held the fervent expectation that some day God would step in and things would get better. The Old Testament was full of promises indicating that they would be a great nation, and their true destiny was to be a world leader. Adversity would only be temporary. In due course God's kingdom would arrive, spearheaded by a Messiah, or deliverer. This ruler, anointed by God himself, would restore his people's ancient faith to its true place, and establish a new order of things in which Jerusalem, its temple and its people would be at the centre of the world stage.

Jesus was not the first person to claim to be the Messiah. As far back as the fifth century BC, some wondered if the Jewish leader Zerubbabel could be the one. More recent times had produced a rash of men claiming they had been selected to play this decisive part in God's ultimate scenario for the life of their nation. Self-styled messiahs were commonplace throughout the first century, both before and after the time of Jesus. It was the emergence of one such figure, Bar Cocheba, that ultimately provoked the Romans to destroy Jerusalem in AD132 and rebuild it as a Greek city from which Jewish people would be excluded.

What was different about Jesus? By any standards, he made a remarkable impact on the lives of his followers. Any would-be leader needs to be a charismatic figure, of course, with the power to move people in such a way that they will make heroic sacrifices for the cause. There are plenty of examples in both ancient and modern history. This kind of fervent devotion usually ends — or is at least diminished — with the death of the leader. Yet it was Jesus' death that mobilized his followers in a way that not only transformed their own lives, but has exercised a remarkable influence on the whole of world history ever since.

How did he achieve this? He had pitifully few resources. According to the Gospels, he and his followers were virtually homeless. None of them shaped up like executive material. Some were rootless bums who had proved inadequate for even such menial posts as they had held. The only thing they all had in common was the fact that they had no influence with people who really counted. No politicians or tycoons. Some could scarcely read and write. Even the brightest were not intellectual geniuses. And what training they received was given in short courses by Jesus himself, as they rested on lonely hillsides or asked questions while wandering from one village to the next. This is not the way to start a multinational corporation.

These people had absolutely nothing going for them. They were typical Galilean peasants. Most had never travelled more than a dozen miles from the place they were born. They were not the kind of people to change the world. Galilee itself was hardly the place to start such an enterprise anyway. Even the urban centres of Palestine were off-limits for the sophisticated intellectuals and military men who ran the Roman Empire. And Galilee was more remote still. Compared with the finesse of people in Greece and Rome, the followers of Jesus were rough and ignorant. They were light years away from the high-sounding rhetoric of the great philosophical schools of the ancient world. Even though they could speak Greek — the universal language of the day — they were not very good at it, and had a strong local dialect. By any standard, their simple homespun belief in Jesus was hardly the stuff that could change empires.

When Jesus was taken into custody by the Romans, and ultimately given the death sentence, they all thought it was the end of the road. But it was just the beginning. In less than twenty years, this small band of people — soon augmented by thousands more — took his message throughout the known world of their day. Growing Christian communities were established in every major population centre in Greece, Asia Minor, Egypt and Italy. Even Rome itself could not dodge their influence. As early as AD48, the Latin writer Suetonius mentioned riots in Rome instigated by someone he calls 'Chrestus'. This was almost certainly a mis-spelling of the name 'Christus' (Christ). The Christian message arrived in Rome with such an impact that people were fighting about it! And it was not long before many upper-class Romans found this new belief absolutely irresistible.

Since the days of Alexander the Great in the fourth century BC, successive governments had tried to unite the Mediterranean world. They had some measure of success. But it was this small and insignificant band of Jesus' followers who laid the foundation for what was to become the greatest unifying force in the whole of European history. Early emperors could see that — and so Nero, Domitian, and others tried to stamp it out. But eventually, the emperor himself became a Christian, and the whole course of world history took a new direction.

What could explain this remarkable achievement? To that question, the first disciples had just one answer. They were convinced that after his death on the cross, Jesus returned to life again. More than that, they were sure that the coming of the Holy Spirit on the Day of Pentecost gave them a new supernatural power in their lives. As a result, they were inspired to remarkable feats of courage and heroism, enduring the most terrifying hardships in order to spread the Christian message. They were certain that their Jesus was not dead, but alive. Their daily experience of the presence of his Spirit convinced them that he was the Messiah of whom the Old Testament had spoken. More than that. Jesus was not merely a great teacher setting a supreme example. He was God himself, and the secrets of the universe could be unlocked only by him.

They did not express their faith in the complex words of the later Christian creeds — they were too simple for that. But the essence of those creeds was certainly there in embryonic form in their thinking. The life, teaching, death, and resurrection of Jesus, together with the coming of the Holy Spirit, was for them the pivotal event of all history. As a result, this one simple life, eked out in poverty among up-country clowns in a place no one had ever heard of, has changed the whole course of world history. We locate ourselves in time and space by reference to the year of his birth. And the whole Western heritage has, in one way and another, been founded on his teaching and the values that he advocated.

If these people were right, then this is the most remarkable life ever lived. If Jesus Christ is God, the power behind the cosmos in a human person, we all need to take him seriously. But can we believe them? Did they actually receive the most momentous revelation of all time — or were they mistaken? That seems a simple question, but it leads into a whole series of profound and far-reaching matters. Can we trust what the Bible tells us about Jesus and his followers? Were his disciples right to think he was the Messiah? Or to conclude that he rose from the dead? And did the Holy Spirit really give them access to some supernatural power for their own lives?

Was Jesus a real person?

Was there such a person as Jesus? Did he exist at all? G.A. Wells is a professor of German at Birkbeck College in London, England. In his book *The Historical Evidence for Jesus*, he claims: 'the earliest references to the historical Jesus are so vague that it is not necessary to hold that he ever existed; the rise of Christianity can ... be explained quite well without him.' The breathtaking boldness of that statement should not blind us to the fact that it is sheer nonsense. It is hard to believe that the New Testament would ever have been written if there was no such person as Jesus. If he had never existed, who would have felt the need to reflect on his significance?

In any case, there is plenty of evidence to show that, whatever we make of him, Jesus was unquestionably a real person. We have already referred to the Roman historian Suetonius. But other writers with more direct knowledge of affairs in Palestine also mention him.

Flavius Josephus was born into an upper-class Jewish family just before the middle of the first century AD. From an early age, he was fascinated by the history and culture of his people. According to his autobiography, he was an expert on Jewish sectarianism at the age of sixteen — and by nineteen he had joined one of the major religious groups, the Pharisees. At the time, Jewish nationalism was coming to the boil, and it was impossible for anyone living in Palestine to keep out of the struggles that would eventually lead to the crushing of Jerusalem by the Roman armies in AD70. Josephus could see some good points in the Romans, and tried to be a peacemaker.

In AD64 he went to Rome to mediate with the Emperor Nero on behalf of some imprisoned priests. There he made friends with Poppaea, the emperor's wife, as a result of which he won his case. This unexpected help, and the magnificence of Rome itself, made a deep impression on him. When he returned home, he tried to promote a policy of peaceful co-existence. But it was too late for that, and before long he found himself in command of a group of freedom fighters in Galilee. In due course he was taken prisoner by the Romans, and brought before the general Vespasian as a prisoner of war. But not for long. In the course of this brief encounter he promised Vespasian that he would soon become the emperor. Not long afterwards, in AD69, he did — and Josephus was set free.

He settled in Rome, and adopted a Roman name. But he was still proud of his roots, and began writing the history of his people. He was determined to show the Romans that the Jews were not really barbarians, as most of them thought. He wrote extensively about the stories of the Old Testament. But he also documented the events of his own century, including a mention of Jesus:

About this time arose Jesus, a wise man, if indeed it be lawful to call him a man. For he was a doer of wonderful deeds, and a teacher of those who gladly receive the truth. He drew to himself many both of the Jews and of the Gentiles . . .

It is short and to the point, and raises some questions about exactly what he knew and believed himself. But it certainly confirms that Josephus had heard of Jesus and believed him to be a real person. And what he says is not inconsistent with the stories in the New Testament Gospels.

The Jewish *Talmud* is a collection of traditional sayings and religious and moral instruction, gathered together over many years. Its authors were certainly no friends of Jesus, but they mention him in similar terms to Josephus. In the same way, the founders of Islam had no hesitation in accepting Luke's Gospel as a true account of Jesus' birth — though, equally, they were unable to accept the New Testament story of his crucifixion.

There is not a single example in the whole of ancient literature of anyone trying to deny that Jesus was a real person. Christians were not always popular in the early Roman Empire, and were accused of some strange things. But no one ever claimed their founder was non-existent. In the face of such unanimous testimony, we may confidently reject the arguments of those who now allege that Christianity was based on a hoax.

Nor is there any dispute about what happened next. History bears eloquent testimony to the fact that Jesus' followers were remarkably successful in convincing others of the truth of their message, and as a result the Roman Empire was changed beyond recognition. Moreover, we have no reason to suppose that any of the earliest Christians were deliberately deceitful or mischievous. Most of them were ordinary people. Writing to a typical group in the middle of the first century — the church at Corinth Paul observed: 'few of you were wise or powerful or of high social standing'. Among the second and third generations of Christian believers, the majority were slaves, many were women, and none of them were people of any importance to the life of the empire. We would never have heard of them had they not met Jesus. Those few who were people of some influence actually gave up a great deal by becoming Christians.

As often as not, following Jesus led to hardship, suffering, ostracism, ridicule — and even, in many cases, death. There was certainly no money to be made out of it: someone like Paul would have been infinitely better off if he had not become a Christian.

With his brilliant mind, he could easily have reached the top of the ladder in his chosen profession. Instead he spent what money he had travelling around the world proclaiming Christ. He willingly gave his all, risking both health and safety. Eventually the paranoid Nero amused himself by coating Christians in tar and using them as torches to light up his front driveway — though since Paul was a Roman citizen, he met his death in a more 'civilized' way by having his head chopped off.

Sane people do not behave in this extraordinary way unless they are absolutely convinced of the truth of the message for which they are willing to give up so much. 'There is no smoke without fire' — and no one would ever have thought to create a religion around Jesus if he had not, at the very least, existed.

7

Finding Jesus in the Gospels

Can we trust the Gospels? This is an important question. Scholars have been debating it at least since the time of the Enlightenment. Some have spent their whole lives searching for the answer, and whole libraries of books have been written. Anything we can say here must be condensed, at least.

We can start by asking where the Gospels actually came from. Some modern writers claim that Jesus was a channeller. He got his information from extra-terrestrials, and communicated it direct to his disciples. The Gospel writers in turn wrote it all down, supplemented by spiritual information channelled through them from their own sources of cosmic consciousness. All this sounds quite attractive to modern pilgrims in search of ultimate answers. Unfortunately, it is not true to the facts. It is certain that Jesus himself neither wrote nor dictated any of the Gospels. Nor is there a shred of evidence to suggest either he or any Gospel writer was a channeller.

Surprisingly, perhaps, there is no absolutely conclusive evidence to show that any of the four New Testament Gospels was written by a direct disciple of Jesus. Two of them (Mark and Luke) certainly were not, though the Gospel of John has a good claim to be substantially the work of the disciple of that name. In any case, the earliest Gospel was written something like twenty to thirty years after Jesus' death. In an age of instant electronic communications, this can seem a definite weakness. But that is a one-sided way of looking at things. Even today the spoken word is the main method of communication for most of the world's people. Even in the West, people are beginning to escape from the rationalist obsession with 'scientific records', and rediscover the contribution of oral history to the proper understanding of the past. All over Europe and North America, projects have been initiated to save in more permanent form the unwritten recollections of older people before their memories fail. It is amazing how comprehensive a power of recall an older person can have, even for events in the dim and distant past. And in cultures where this form of memorizing is encouraged and promoted, oral reminiscences provide an exceedingly accurate way of recording history.

A striking example of this is the story of the black American Alex Haley, who went searching for his ancestors in the 1970s. They were slaves, of course, and for that reason there was little substantial documentary evidence for their early life in America. But there was enough to piece together a coherent picture. Bills, receipts, lists of slaves and their children, together with stories handed on to him by his grandmother — who had learned them from her mother and grandmother — these were the raw materials for Haley's investigations. Using them, he succeeded in recreating his family story right back to the point where the first person had stepped on to American soil. But the written evidence stopped there. Beyond that, all he had to go on was the story he had heard from his grandmother.

The story began with his ancestor being captured not far from an African village, being cruelly manacled and then transported from the shores of West Africa across to the other side of the Atlantic. Would that be enough for a modern American to retrace the voyage of the slave traders to Africa, and find the tribe from which he was descended? It seemed an impossible dream. But with nothing more than the oral recollections of his grandmother to guide him, Haley set out for Africa. The information he had — all based on stories passed on by word of mouth for almost 200 years — seemed to point to a particular area of the Gambia. There were no written records there either for a time so long in the past. But imagine Haley's surprise — and delight — when the oral history told by the elders of a local tribe turned out to dovetail exactly into the stories he had learned from his grandmother on the other side of the world!

Alex Haley's oral family history took him back a couple of centuries. By contrast, the oral period for the New Testament stories about Jesus covers something like fifty years at most. Some of it a lot less. For instance, at the beginning of 1 Corinthians chapter 15 Paul mentions some eyewitness evidence about the resurrection of Jesus.

He actually wrote this down in about AD55. But he says he had known the information since he first became a Christian. And that happened not more than a year or two after Jesus' death. Compared with other written accounts about persons and events in the Roman world, we are far closer to eyewitnesses here than anywhere else.

But there is another question. This time addressed to us. What do we expect to find in the Gospels? History? Biography? Chronological accounts? Word-for-word precision in reporting what Jesus said? Or something else? The Gospel writers themselves use none of this language to describe their books. The only thing they all consistently claim is that they are writing 'the good news'. That is what the word 'gospel' means. Now to describe anything as 'good' news is to make a value judgment on it. To commend it, to affirm that those who read it will be glad that they did. Two of the Gospel writers come clean and admit this quite openly. John says in chapter 20 of his Gospel that he hopes that as a result of reading his book, others may 'believe that Jesus is the Messiah, the Son of God, and that through your faith in him, you may have life'. He discloses that he has selected the stories that would be most useful for this purpose from a vast body of other information available to him. Luke begins his account by saying that he too worked in the same way. To start with, he read what others had written about Jesus, and then made his own selection. He also opted for some stories in preference to others 'so that you will know the full truth about everything which you have been taught'.

We can see right away that the Gospels contain only selected episodes from Jesus' life. Fully half of Mark is taken up with the very last week of Jesus' life. There is nothing about his birth or childhood, and only a brief mention of the resurrection. None of the Gospels mention Jesus' early childhood, nor do they even tell us what he looked like. And putting together everything that is contained in all four would not produce anything like enough material to fill up every day in the three years which they do describe! Whatever they were trying to do, these people were not aiming for a comprehensive account of the whole of Jesus' life.

Does this mean the Gospel writers were biased, then? Of course they were. They all believed in Jesus. Through his teaching they had discovered new purpose for their own everyday existence, and they wanted to share that with other people. They were convinced that Jesus was not dead, but alive, and was now continuing his work through the supernatural power of the Holy Spirit in his people. These writers were more than just biased: they were certain that the absolute truth about life's meaning was to be found in Jesus. If they had not been, they would never have bothered to write about him at all.

No doubt some readers will be thinking this proves what they have long suspected. How can people so biased possibly present an objective picture? But who says that only supposedly 'unbiased' people can ever tell the truth? Indeed, is there such a thing as an 'unbiased' person? Every day in life we all receive information that comes to us from many different sources. To know anything at all about events we have not witnessed ourselves, we all depend on the accounts of those who did. And those accounts are invariably 'biased'. Can you believe what you read in the newspapers? Or what you see on television? Seeing things for ourselves on the small screen should be more reliable. But even that generally presents only a partial view of things. For most of the 1980s, Iran and Iraq were locked in a terrifying military conflict. But what was actually going on? Our television screens showed pictures from the battlefield every day. But the impressions we gained depended entirely on which side of the lines the camera took the pictures. Then the way the reports were edited and shown reflected the political sympathies of the particular channel. If you or I had been there, our reports would have exhibited our own partialities.

In everyday life, we take all this for granted. Indeed, we actually expect people to explain to us the significance of what they report. This is what distinguishes news reports and 'proper history' from bare data. Mere records contain 'facts' — but in an abstract and incoherent way. Suppose you ask me what my wife is like. I could reply by giving you her date of birth, her height, the colour of her hair and eyes, and so on. But what will that tell you about her? Before she becomes even remotely interesting as a living person you want to hear a few stories — typical episodes that highlight her attitudes and define her outlook. You would look for value judgments as well, and even if I included totally subjective concepts like love you would still get a good idea of what she is really like. By all means, I would be a 'biased' witness. But the fact that I am giving my own personal perceptions does not of itself make my information unreliable. Quite the reverse, for this sort of impressionistic account is normally far more enlightening than 'brute facts'.

I was once run down by a car in the streets of Edinburgh, Scotland. I was not seriously injured, but since I was on a crossing controlled by traffic signals, the driver was duly summoned to appear in court. I had to go and give evidence — to tell the story as I had experienced it. I was not the only one to do so. My wife told hers. The prosecutor told his — along with the defence lawyer, the car driver and others who witnessed the scene. A policeman was also called to present evidence. He spoke of the condition of the road surface and described the weather at the time, as well as giving an account of the precise width of the road, the car's dimensions, and how all that related to where I was standing when the car struck me. Whatever else he said, he was undoubtedly recording the 'bare facts'. My recollections were completely different, and certainly did not include things like the dimensions of the car or the road. The driver's story was different again.

When the judge reached his decision, he took all this into account. He did not say, 'Because I have heard several stories of what happened, this accident cannot possibly have taken place.' Nor did he go on to conclude that there was a fair chance that the car and the road — even Edinburgh itself — did not exist either. To do so would have been absurd, and we all know that. Yet this is exactly the sort of crazy conclusion that otherwise intelligent people seem prepared to reach when talking about the New Testament. The four Gospels are not word-for-word the same, we say; their writers were biased; they make value judgments about what they report. So the only safe conclusion must be that these things never happened, and maybe Jesus never existed! If we lived our everyday lives on this set of assumptions, we would all be in a big mess.

The Gospel writers were actually far more sophisticated than we give them credit for. Luke wrote a follow-up volume to link the story of Jesus to the story of his early disciples. This is the book of Acts. One of the striking things about it is that it tells the same story three times. Paul's dramatic spiritual experience on the road to Damascus appears in Acts chapters 9, 22 and 26. And all three versions are different. Why? Because Luke had no idea what actually happened? Because he was making it all up?

If he had been doing that, he would certainly not have produced three distinctive versions. As it is, he adapts the same story at different points in his narrative to present varied aspects of the meaning of what he reports. If one writer could do that within a single book, why should we be surprised when different writers utilize the stories about Jesus in diverse ways?

If modern readers find this hard to accept, it is because they are imprisoned by their own presuppositions about how the Gospels should have been written. The Gospel writers were not interested in preserving the words of Jesus merely as souvenirs from the past. They were not primarily ancient historians. For them, Jesus' teaching was a living message, with the power to bring new light into the lives of those who read and reflected on it. It was something to be used, not merely recorded. Even something as important as the Lord's Prayer was used in different forms when Christians met for worship — and so Matthew's version was not quite identical with Luke's. After both their Gospels had been written, continued use changed it a bit more, adding the ascription of glory with which all modern versions now conclude!

Those who criticize the Gospel writers on these grounds are just being unfair by imposing standards of logical consistency that would never be applied to any other literature.

This is all circumstantial evidence. But the case for the general authenticity of the Gospels rests on other solid considerations as well.

Remember for a start that ancient people were just as conscious of the need for proper research as we are today. They used different tools and procedures to verify their information.

But they did not make things up. It is only intellectual imperialism that suspects a book just because it is ancient. Latin and Greek historians had high standards and sophisticated techniques for sifting and assessing their information. Luke and John both indicate they used the same procedures, and there is every reason to think the others did the same.

In addition, the Gospel stories show direct and specific knowledge of life in Palestine at the time of Jesus. Yet some Gospel writers were certainly not at home in Palestine, and one (Luke) was not a Jew. They were all writing after the events they describe, at a time when the face of the country had been irreversibly changed by the devastation of a major war. And they compiled their books in places geographically far removed from the scene of Jesus' ministry. They must have been relying on information that went back much further in time and was based on actual knowledge of the places and people mentioned. Such archaeological finds as there have been show the Gospel writers to have been correct even in cases where they were once thought to be mistaken. A hundred years ago, it was often said that John had simply imagined some of the places he mentions in Jerusalem. Sites such as the Pool of Bethesda or Pilate's 'Pavement' must have some symbolic meaning rather than being real places. Or so it was claimed. But fresh knowledge about the city at the time of Jesus has demonstrated that such ideas were mistaken. John's information comes from somebody who knew Jerusalem, and had been there at the time of Jesus' own visits.

There is also the fact that behind the teachings of Jesus (recorded in the Gospels in Greek) we can trace clear echoes of the language of rural Palestine: Aramaic. This was the everyday tongue of home and market-place, and though Jesus could probably speak Greek, much of his teaching would be given in Aramaic. Even the Gospels written in Greek occasionally preserve Aramaic expressions — like the words from the cross found in Matthew chapter 27, or the call to Jairus's daughter in chapter 5 of Mark, or the name of 'the Pavement' in Jerusalem used in chapter 19 of John. At other points, notably in the Sermon on the Mount in Matthew chapters 5 to 7, when sayings of Jesus are translated back into Aramaic they display literary features that would only have made sense in that language. Facts such as these do not of course 'prove' that Jesus spoke these words. But they unquestionably take us back into the culture of Jesus himself — and the nearer we are to his own time, the greater our confidence in trusting their authenticity.

Another striking fact is that the Gospels are different in every way from the rest of the New Testament. Different in form, for much of the rest consists of letters written by various Christian leaders to their friends. But different also in fundamental concerns. Very soon after Jesus' death there was a wide-ranging controversy over the relationship between Jews and non-Jews in the Christian community. Put in a nutshell, did a Gentile need to convert to Judaism in order to be a true follower of Jesus? This was a crucial practical issue, for Jews and non-Jews needed to get along with each other in the church, and their habits were often quite different. But it was a theological question too, for if Jesus was the Messiah, then how did being one of his followers relate to those who were part of the people of God in the faith stemming from the Old Testament?

Church leaders wrestled with that question for a long time. If only Jesus had said something on it, much heart-searching and acrimony could have been avoided. There must have been great pressure for somebody to invent a 'saying of Jesus' that would provide the definitive answer! The amazing thing is that there is no sign of that happening. Nor do the Gospels have anything to say about other key concerns of the early church. Baptism and teachings about church membership hardly feature at all, and two major Gospel themes — the kingdom of God and the Son of Man — are scarcely mentioned at all in the rest of the New Testament.

The only reasonable conclusion to draw is that the Gospels give us an authentic picture of Jesus as he actually was. Not a photographic record — but then they never claimed to do that. Nor an exact word-for-word account of all his teaching. But they do not claim that either. They are more like portraits than photographs. We see Jesus through the eyes of those who knew his teaching and admired his example. Far from invalidating their stories, this very fact itself makes what they have written more true to life — and more accessible to us.

'Secret' Gospels

So far so good. But do Matthew, Mark, Luke and John actually portray the real Jesus? They may be true enough — as far as they go. But are they one-sided? Doctored versions of the real thing, published by the early church leaders to back up their own beliefs? Is what they left out even more important than what they put in? Were there other 'Gospels'? And if so, what do they tell us about Jesus?

In December 1960, Professor Morton Smith of Columbia University, New York, gave an address to the American Society of Biblical Literature. The proceedings of such an exalted body of egg-heads would not normally be noticed by the popular press. But this was different. Morton Smith had been working on some academic project in the library of Mar Saba monastery, not far from Jerusalem. While he was there, he came across a letter scribbled in Greek inside the covers of a book containing the letters of Ignatius. He was a church leader at Antioch early in the second century AD. But this particular copy of his writings was not ancient, and had been printed in Amsterdam in 1646. The handwriting in the letter was even more recent than that — probably about the middle of the eighteenth century. But it claimed to be a copy of a letter originally written by Clement of Alexandria, a prominent Christian thinker towards the end of the second century.

The letter claims that after Mark wrote his Gospel in Rome he made his way to Alexandria in Egypt. There he produced a second edition. The original (New Testament) Gospel had given just a simple account of the life and teachings of Jesus. But this second edition was for more advanced believers, and contained more 'spiritual' teachings. The letter makes a vague mention of a young man who came to Jesus and stayed overnight with him. It describes a secret initiation ceremony that took place, with the character of a hypnotic out-of-the-body experience that is described in terms similar to the story of Jesus' transfiguration in Mark chapter 9. In the course of this experience, the initiate discovered 'the mystery of the Kingdom of God', presumably secret teachings such as this expanded version of Mark allegedly contained.

The letter is only a single scrap of paper. Some experts think it could have been the work of Clement, though others suspect it may be a hoax. In any case, no one has yet produced a copy of this enlarged edition of Mark. But there are plenty of other documents from the third and fourth centuries that also claim to contain secret teachings of Jesus.

Their existence has been known for a long time. Church leaders from the second to the fourth centuries mention such 'Gospels' in their own writings, usually identifying them as the work of 'Gnostics'. But it is only in modern times that actual copies have come to light. In 1769 two 'books of Jeu' written in Coptic turned up near the Egyptian city of Thebes. A few years later, in 1785, the British Museum acquired Coptic manuscripts of two books called *Pistis-Sophia*. However, it was well into the nineteenth century before it began to dawn on anyone what they were all about. Even then, there was no adequate frame of reference in which they could be properly understood.

In 1896, a few more Coptic texts were discovered in Egypt. These included mysterious-sounding titles such as *The Apocryphon of John*, *The Sophia of Jesus Christ*, *The Acts of Peter*, and *The Gospel of Mary*. A German professor by the name of Carl Schmidt made plans to translate and publish them. But just as they were about to go to press, a burst water pipe in the printer's cellar ruined the plates. The work was put on one side, and it was well into the second half of the twentieth century before they were ready to be published — by which time their usefulness had been largely superseded. A few fragments of papyrus manu-scripts containing teachings of Jesus were also discovered at the beginning of this century at Oxyrhynchus. But it was just after World War II that the largest and most valuable collection of such writings came to light.

Towards the end of 1945, a camel driver by the name of Mohammed Ali El-Samman was digging for manure at the foot of the cliffs of Gebel et Tarif, not far from the modern town of Nag Hammadi in Upper Egypt. Piles of decomposed bird drop-pings there provide a regular source of compost for local farmers. While he was scooping it up, Mohammed uncovered a large jar. Inside, he found a collection of papyrus leaves, bound like books between leather covers. They were in Coptic — a language he did not understand — so he took them along to the priest of the local Coptic church. He could not read them either, as they were not in the medieval church Coptic with which he was familiar.

The documents seemed to be of little value. But there was no harm in hoping, and Mohammed set about trying to market them through an underground network of antique dealers with whom he had dealt before. Within a year, they were spotted in Cairo by a man called Togo Mina. He was director of the Coptic Museum, and on 4 October 1946 he succeeded in purchasing some of the papyrus sheets. By chance, a letter from France landed on his desk at about the same time. It was from a young scholar by the name of Jean Doresse. He and his wife Marianne had a keen interest in the history and literature of the ancient Coptic church, and they were planning to visit Egypt to explore the sites of some ancient monasteries.

They arrived in late summer 1947. It was a dream come true for them both. But when they got to Egypt, they found the country in the grip of a savage cholera epidemic, which made it extremely risky for them to travel anywhere except the major cities. Instead of visiting the remote areas that most interested them, they went to see Togo Mina at the Coptic Museum. Jean and Marianne both wanted to see the extensive collections of papyrus documents, paintings, statues, jewellery, and other objects remaining from the Coptic Christian culture of the early centuries. Besides, Mina had already written to them, saying that he was eager to meet them. As they walked up the tree-lined drive of the beige plastered museum — surrounded on all sides by the remains of many different civilizations — they had no idea what awaited them inside. But it was not what they expected.

They were ushered straight into the director's private office. There, he opened a drawer of his large desk, and produced a bundle of papyrus sheets, written in Coptic, bound between soft leather covers. The same sheets he had bought from a dealer some months earlier, and which had originally come from the dung heap at Nag Hammadi. Jean and Marianne could see they were special. For these were Gnostic texts. Five of them in all, and including accounts of conversations between Jesus and his disciples. There was also a copy of the documents that had come to light in 1896, but which had never been published.

The French visitors were fascinated, and wanted to see more. Before long they persuaded Togo Mina to set up a meeting with Albert Eid. He was a well-known Belgian antique dealer living in Cairo, and word had it that he possessed some other similar manuscripts. These turned out to be more dog-eared. But they included something called *The Gospel of Truth*, as well as a letter about resurrection addressed to a person by the name of Rheginos, together with other assorted materials. Eid knew that others were also circulating on the black market. And he finally disclosed where they had come from. The Doresses could hardly contain their excitement when he mentioned the village of Hamra Dom, for that was the very place they had been hoping to visit. By now the cholera was under control, and it was safe to make a short trip there. But if the villagers knew anything, they were not telling.

Not long after they got back to France, Jean and Marianne heard that more texts had turned up on the black market. Jean returned to Cairo immediately. By this time, however, Egypt was at war with the newly created state of Israel. That, combined with the suspicion of the dealers who had the texts, meant he was able to catch no more than a glimpse of them. But that was enough. He recorded in his diary that they had 'sensationally attractive titles'. Names like the *Gospel of Philip*, the *Gospel of Thomas*, the *Letter of Peter to Philip*, not to mention the *Revelation of Adam to his son Seth*. Still nothing could persuade the dealers to part with these priceless manuscripts. By now they knew their true value, and feared the Egyptian government would confiscate them and give nothing at all in return. So they were smuggled out of the country and taken to New York. Surprisingly, no one there was interested, and they had to be smuggled back to Egypt again!

Cloak-and-dagger dealings like this went on for several years. Repeated efforts to do a deal with the Egyptian government all fell through. Scholars were desperate to get their hands on the texts, and some managed to acquire transcripts of them. One entire document even found its way to Germany, where it was presented as a gift to the famous psychiatrist Carl Jung. But the majority of them remained in Cairo, unceremoniously dumped in an old suitcase until someone could be persuaded to come up with the right sort of cash. It was 1956 before the Coptic Museum finally succeeded in recovering them all, including the one from Germany which by now had been given the name *The Jung Codex*.

Compared with the mysteries surrounding their discovery, the actual contents of these texts was fairly straightforward. This small library turned out to contain fifty-two separate works, contained in thirteen volumes. It is not certain who first collected them, but there was no problem finding out when they were written. Bits of scrap papyrus had been stuffed inside the covers as strengthening. They included invoices, receipts, letters, and so on — and they all had dates between AD333 and 348. That means the books were probably bound about AD350, and hidden away not long after.

So what about these 'Gospels'? Do they contain an alternative message of Jesus? Perhaps even his 'real' teaching, which was disowned by the leaders of the early church and had lain unread until their discovery in modern times?

We certainly know that many sayings of Jesus were left out of the New Testament Gospels. The New Testament writers themselves said that what they used had been extracted from much larger collections known to them. So in principle there is no particular reason why some of this other material should not have been preserved elsewhere. It would be surprising if it had not. The *Gospel of Thomas* contains 114 sayings of Jesus. The vast majority of them are very similar to well-known New Testament passages. But they are not the same. Does *Thomas* contain expansions and additions? Or is it the New Testament Gospels that have serious omissions?

If we could be sure that *Thomas* was compiled as early as some of the New Testament Gospels, then that would be a genuine question. As it is, however, *Thomas* in its present form seems to date from about the fourth century. And no one doubts that it is a thoroughly Gnostic text. It was probably translated into Coptic from Greek, and by coincidence some of its sayings are found not only in the New Testament, but also (in Greek) in the papyrus documents discovered earlier this century at Oxyrhynchus. When we compare these three versions of Jesus' teaching, it becomes obvious that the sayings in *Thomas* are a development based on the New Testament, and not some form of 'independent' — still less 'more reliable' — Gospel.

Consider the following statements that are found in all three sources. From Matthew Chapter 7: 'Seek and you will find . . . he who seeks finds.' From Matthew chapter 11: 'Come to me and I will give you rest.' From Oxyrhynchus Papyrus 654: 'Let him who seeks not cease seeking until he finds; and when he finds he will be astounded, and having been astounded he will reign; and reigning, he will rest.' From the *Gospel of Thomas* saying 2: 'He who seeks should not stop seeking until he finds; and when he finds, he will be bewildered; and when he is bewildered, he will marvel, and will reign over the All.'

You do not need to be a Coptic scholar to see how the relatively simple New Testament saying has developed through the half-way house of Oxyrhynchus into the Gnostic version found in *Thomas*. At those points where it can be tested, *Thomas* — and other similar 'Gospels' — has clearly imposed an interpretation on the sayings it contains, in order to give them a meaning congenial to the members of the sect who preserved it. Moreover, this understanding coincides with the relative dates at which the various documents were written: the New Testament in the first century, the Oxyrhynchus finds at the end of the second, and *Thomas* (at least in its Nag Hammadi version) about the beginning of the fourth. Claims that *Thomas* or any other Gnostic Gospels contain the 'real teaching' of Jesus are nothing more than imagination and wishful thinking.

But who were these Gnostics, who needed their own Gospels to back up their beliefs? We met one of them, Marcion, briefly in Chapter 3. Now is the time to set them in a broader context.

Christians have often assumed that the time of Jesus and his immediate disciples was some sort of golden age in the church's life. A time when everyone thought exactly the same as everyone else, and there was one totally unified church. The modern ecumenical movement has often proceeded on that assumption, believing that the different denominations in today's church are a falling away from an original state of complete unity within the Christian faith. But the facts are not that simple. Apart from anything else, every modern denomination claims to be legitimately descended from the church of New Testament times. And they are probably right. All of them.

There has always been diversity in the life of the church. The New Testament reflects this very clearly. Half of it consists of letters written by Paul to other Christians who expressed their faith in Christ using terms different from those he felt comfortable with. Yet all these people had a legitimate place somewhere in the mainstream of church life. Paul never implies they were not 'real Christians' — and some of their diverse points of view also found their way into the New Testament. The letter of James, for example, is not saying exactly the same things as Paul. James may even be quoting Paul in one passage (James chapter 2 verses 18 to 24) — in order to disagree with him!

Almost from the very beginning, Christianity had at least two forms: Jewish and Gentile. Two 'denominations', if you like. Jewish Christians stressed the continuity of the church with Judaism. They believed Jesus was the Messiah — the Messiah of the Jewish people — and therefore to follow Jesus automatically involved the acceptance of Judaism. All Jews kept the various laws of the Old Testament, especially circumcision (for men) and the regulations about food. Jewish Christians did the same, and when they organized their own churches they instinctively adopted the patterns they knew in the synagogue.

The Gentile denomination started with Jewish believers too. They also believed that Jesus was the Messiah, and that the experience of his followers was continuous with life of the people of God as documented in the Old Testament. But they could not see how that required Gentile people to join the Jewish religion in order to be Christians. For them, Judaism had been transformed. Keeping the Law in all its details was no longer necessary. Believers in Jesus had been set free from all that, they argued — and their freedom found expression in their own distinctive pattern of church organization, as they adopted the more 'charismatic' model championed especially by Paul.

The origins of this diversity were simple. Different circumstances demand answers to different questions. Sometimes, different answers to the same questions. Christians in a modern Western city will not express their faith in exactly the same way as their counterparts in a tribal culture in south-east Asia. The Roman world was just the same. Life in Jerusalem was not identical with life in a Greek city such as Corinth. Rome was different again. As Jesus' followers moved out with their message, Christian groups sprang up in all these places. They shared a core of central beliefs. They all accepted Jesus was the Messiah promised in the Hebrew scriptures. They all believed he was a full and perfect expression of the character of God himself. God in a human person — the 'Son of God'. And they were all convinced that after his death on the cross he returned from death, and made God's supernatural power available to his followers through the presence of the Holy Spirit. But they all had their favourite ways of expressing these beliefs — both in their thinking and in their daily lifestyle.

Judaism always had a diverse structure. The Pharisees and Sadducees mentioned in the New Testament were two quite distinct groups. And we know there were others. Judaism encompassed a wide spectrum of faith, and when Jewish people became followers of Jesus, the spectrum was enlarged to include 'Jewish Christians'. In the days following the resurrection of Jesus, his disciples worshipped happily in the temple and synagogues of Jerusalem. From Acts chapter 15 verse 5 we can see that even later it was perfectly possible to be a Christian and a Pharisee at the same time. Sociologically, one section of the early church was a type of reformed Judaism.

There was a similar set-up in the wider Roman world. Here there were many religious groupings loosely connected with one another, including traditional Greek and Roman religion as well as recent arrivals such as the mysteries. People from these circles were attracted in large numbers to the growing churches in Greek and Roman cities. They naturally brought their own intellectual baggage with them, and this often caused problems. In Corinth, Paul had a desperate time trying to identify the core of authentic Christian belief and to unravel it from the other inherited ideas that many converts still held.

In the long term, it proved impossible to hold this wide spectrum together. Pagans themselves became less tolerant of Christians, whom they regarded as 'atheists' because they would worship only one God. The Jews also lost patience with the Christians. Judaism itself was going through an identity crisis, and the last thing the rabbis wanted was a splinter group giving allegiance to Jesus as Messiah. By the end of the first century Christians were officially barred from membership of the synagogues, and in a short time the Jewish Christian churches had disappeared. It became necessary for Christians to define their beliefs and practices with greater precision. The mainstream of the church emerged as Catholic Christianity — the traditional church. But other streams regrouped as they tried to come to terms with the new situation.

Gnosticism was one of the major fringe groups on the Gentile side of the church, though it also had some contacts with Judaism. The Gnostics were not a single group. Many different sects have been loosely associated for convenience under this one title. No two groups thought exactly the same. But they all had some common features that distinguished them from mainstream Christianity.

Their beliefs were based on the conviction that there is not one world, but two. The world of spirit, where God is, which is holy and pure; and the world of matter, where we are, which is evil and corrupt. If God is holy and pure, they reasoned, then there is no way he can have any dealings with our world. Our only hope is to escape to the spiritual world and find true fulfilment there. The chance to escape comes at death. But not everyone is qualified to reach the world of spirit. To do so, a person must have a divine 'spark' embedded in their nature, otherwise they will return to the world to start another meaningless round of bodily existence. Even those who have the 'spark' cannot be certain of finding ultimate release, for the evil creators of this world jealously guard every escape route to the world of spirit. To outwit them, mere possession of the divine spark is not enough. The spark must be enlightened about its own nature and the character of true salvation — and for this it requires 'knowledge' (*gnosis*). Not an intellectual knowledge, but a mystical illumination: a direct 'knowing' of the supreme God. Many Gnostics believed the secret of this knowledge had been given to a chosen few by a divine redeemer who descended into this world from the spirit world. Some identified this redeemer with Jesus.

Ideas like this are widespread in the history of religions. Hinduism is so similar that some have claimed there was a link between it and ancient Gnosticism. The search for personal fulfilment through union with some cosmic consciousness is a major preoccupation for many serious spiritual searchers in the modern world. Weary of the dead-end answers to life's problems proposed by rationalists, millions of people are now looking for salvation and personal release through a mystical experience of enlightenment which is not so very different from the ancient Gnostic concept of 'knowledge'.

The exact origins of Gnosticism are still something of a mystery. Most of our evidence relates to Christian forms. It also existed in other, non-Christian forms. But one thing we can be certain of: Gnosticism was certainly not the original form of Christianity. Gnostics were willing to utilize and adapt certain elements of Jesus' teaching — just as they did with concepts from many other religions. But they could never accept the central conviction of Jesus' earliest disciples. Gnostics found it impossible to believe that Jesus could be a manifestation of God in a human person. One leading Gnostic, Cerinthus, suggested that a divine force had entered the human Jesus at his baptism, and then left him again before the crucifixion. That way he was able to accept Jesus as a revealer of spiritual secrets, while avoiding the idea that God was either born or died as a human person.

This was also a problem for Islamic teachers, and some early Muslim literature claims that it was not really Jesus who died on the cross. Other stories suggest that Jesus went on to live the rest of his life in relative obscurity in India, where he died in old age. Modern visitors to the subcontinent can actually see what is claimed to be his tomb at Khanyar Street in Sirinagar, India — along with the alleged grave of his mother Mary in Muree, Pakistan. But none of this is a serious addition to our historical knowledge of Jesus. The New Testament Gospels were written only a couple of decades after the events they describe, and it makes no sense to pass them over in favour of other traditions that developed six or seven centuries later.

Stories such as these are motivated by embarrassment with the claim that Jesus was both truly God and truly human, combined with the belief that a transcendent God could not become directly involved in the affairs of this mundane world. But the earliest witnesses of Jesus' life and teaching had no such difficulties. For them, God was not isolated from this world. He is its Creator, and the material world is fundamentally good. God cares for men and women in the affairs of everyday life, they declared. Salvation is not escaping from the world, but meeting God in it — especially in the life, death and resurrection of Jesus, who was both fully divine and fully human.

Proof of the resurrection

The resurrection of Jesus was the one thing that convinced the first Christians of the truth of all this. Writing in the mid-fifties of the first century, Paul claimed in 1 Corinthians chapter 15 that 'if Christ has not been raised, then your faith is a delusion . . . ' The idea that Jesus rose from death is certainly the most extraordinary feature of all the stories about him. And one that raises many questions for people today.

Helmut Koester was at one time a professor at Harvard Divinity School, and is now a Lutheran bishop. According to him, none of Jesus' original disciples ever thought of believing he had risen to life again. Belief in the resurrection was a late idea, he claims, only coming to prominence after the Christians had been forced to leave Jerusalem at the time of the Jewish revolt against the Romans (AD66-70). Up until then, they regularly met for worship at the tomb of Jesus. But what could they do once they had been barred from entering the city? To answer that question, the story of the empty tomb was put together to explain why, after all, they did not need to worship there.

Worship at the tombs of heroes is a common practice. It happened in Jesus' day (see Matthew chapter 23 verse 29), and modern visitors to Israel can still join throngs of worshippers at the tombs of Abraham in Hebron, of David in Jerusalem, and of some of the ancient rabbis as well. Nowadays, lines of Christian pilgrims also make their way to the Church of the Resurrection, and the Garden Tomb. But to suggest that the discontinuation of such a practice in the first century led to belief that Jesus was alive is completely far-fetched. For one thing, there is no evidence that anybody at all was interested in the place where Jesus was buried earlier than the fourth century. In addition, we have the statements made by Paul in 1 Corinthians, written at least ten years before AD66. One Gospel had certainly been written by then — probably more. And these accounts were undoubtedly based on stories that went right back into the earliest days of the church. It makes no sense at all to suggest that the resurrection belief was a late development. The fact is that Christians did not venerate the tomb of Jesus because they believed there was nothing in it. And they held this belief right from the start.

But were they right? All the Gospels say that three days after his burial Jesus' tomb was empty. But they do not all tell the same story. This may appear to be an argument against their reliability. It is actually a strong argument on the other side. Remember my experience at the Sheriff Court in Edinburgh? Eyewitnesses often give very different accounts of what they have seen, even when it is something as commonplace as a traffic accident. Imagine how they might have coped with something as remarkable as a dead person coming to life again. The disciples themselves no more expected such a thing to happen than you or I would. According to Mark chapter 9, the very notion of 'resurrection' was alien to their whole way of thinking. Is it surprising that they did not tell a logical and coherent story? If such an unbelievable story had been made up, we might reasonably expect they would have made sure that it at least sounded consistent. And what ancient writer would ever have invented a story in which the main witnesses were women — people who were generally given no credence at all as witnesses to anything? For all its variations, the evidence unequivocally points to the fact that Jesus' body disappeared from its tomb. This is what the Jewish scholar, Geza Vermes, writes in his book Jesus the Jew:

When every argument has been considered and weighed, the only conclusion acceptable to the historian must be . . . that the women who set out to pay their last respects to Jesus found to their consternation, not a body, but an empty tomb.

Why then was the tomb empty? The New Testament supplements the story of the empty tomb with a series of other stories in which the 'risen' Jesus allegedly appeared to various people. What can we make of these? Perhaps these people were mistaken? They thought they were meeting their dead master, miraculously raised back to life. But at best they were having visions — at worst, perhaps, hallucinations. The ancient world knew of all these possibilities. Certain cults laid a premium on worshippers having an experience in which deities such as Isis and Asclepius appeared to their devotees. But such visions were not quite the same as those the Christians thought they had. These were mythical figures from the long forgotten past, so nobody really knew what they looked like anyway. But Jesus was well-known to the disciples. He had died not long before. They would know if it was him all right. In addition, his appearances just happened, whereas these other alleged visions of gods were produced to order by the use of various well-tried hypnotic rituals.

Several facts make it unlikely that the disciples were the victims of some sort of psychological trick. If Jesus' tomb was empty, only three lots of people could have removed his body: the Jews, the Romans, or the disciples themselves. Jews and Romans both had a vested interest in squashing the Christian message. They could have done so by producing a body, if they had one. Since they did not, we may presume that they had not taken it. So what about the disciples? They were prepared to stake their lives on the fact that Jesus was alive. Many of them were brutally murdered for their faith, including Peter and other members of Jesus' inner circle, who would be prime suspects for removing the body. It is simply impossible to believe they would willingly suffer in this way if all the time they knew where they themselves had hidden Jesus' body.

The nature of the appearances themselves have none of the signs of hallucinatory experiences. Paul's evidence is of special value, for unlike the others he was psychically experienced. He

writes in 2 Corinthians chapter 12 of having had visions and
revelations of a mystical nature on several occasions. But he placed
his Damascus road encounter with the risen Jesus in a different
category altogether.

Jesus Son of God

On his own confession, Paul was an ardent Jew. He was well
satisfied with living and believing as a Pharisee. The thing that
changed his mind was his own meeting with the risen Jesus. He had
been looking for the coming Messiah. But the whole course of Jesus'
life seemed to show quite conclusively that he was nothing but a
discredited and disreputable pretender. On the Damascus road,
Paul discovered he was wrong. Not only was Jesus the Messiah:
he also turned out to be God's Son. Before that, Paul could never
have entertained the idea that anyone else could stand alongside
God. Greeks and Romans might use the extravagant language of
divine sonship to describe emperors and other heroes. But Paul,
like the rest of his race, was fiercely monotheistic. As a Christian,
he still believed in only one God — but now he was convinced that
God could only be fully known through Jesus. More than that, he
even used the title that the Old Testament had reserved exclusively
for God himself — 'Lord' — and applied it to Jesus. Jesus was 'the
Lord', and no one, wrote Paul in Romans chapter 10, could be a
Christian without believing that.

Jesus had not used the sophisticated terminology developed by
Paul and others, but he certainly made claims that amounted to
the same thing. He always addressed God as 'Father', using an
Aramaic word that would only have been acceptable in the close
familiarity of the family (*Abba*). Regular Jewish prayers were much
more dignified, and to use such a word would have been a mark of
irreverence. It was too casual and intimate. Jesus knew that. But he
still used it. He thought it was appropriate — presumably because
he believed he had the right to be intimate with God. He actually
was God's Son!

We have come a long way since we began our search for the real
Jesus. Half-way round the ancient world, and along a few byways
in our own. What have we discovered? Nothing very startling,
perhaps. If the real Jesus is to be found, then we need to go to
the New Testament Gospels to find him. Despite loud claims to

the contrary, these are still the only sources of authentic knowledge about this remarkable person. But their striking portrait of him leads on to yet more questions. This time about the very meaning of life itself. For if Jesus did truly conquer death, if he was actually God's Son, and if he holds the key to the secrets of the cosmos, then we must press on to try and discover what relevance it all has to life at the end of the twentieth century.

8
Searching for a New Future

Since the very beginning of time, people have asked themselves the ultimate questions. Why are we here? What does life mean? How long can it last? What happens after death? And a thousand other imponderables. Philosophers and sages of every generation have thought they knew the answers. Some things would always be changing. But others were permanent. Like the earth itself. The philosopher of the Old Testament, the writer of the book of Ecclesiastes, put it this way: 'Generations come and generations go, but the world stays just the same.' Today, however, no one can say that. It is not just the world's people who face a crisis of existence: it is the earth itself.

Humanity has always been poised on a knife-edge. Disease has decimated whole populations not only in the developing world in our own generation, but as far back as the Middle Ages, when plagues rampaged uncontrollably through the great cities of Europe. War is nothing new either. We have been killing each other since the dawn of history. Only now we can do it with greater sophistication and enhanced efficiency. But as we approach the beginning of a new millennium, we are faced with a crisis of frightening proportions. We are slowly destroying our planet. Two hundred years ago, in the heady days of the Industrial Revolution, it seemed as if the human race had finally gained the upper hand. As technology developed at a rapidly increasing pace, fuelled by the philosophical fires of Enlightenment optimism, life gradually became more comfortable for the world's people. The belief that the cosmos operates according to fixed laws of nature, and that progress consists in understanding and harnessing those laws, has undoubtedly produced some spectacular gains from which we have all benefited.

World in crisis

But scientists can no longer talk optimistically of the future. The idea that technology can resolve all our problems is not a popular doctrine nowadays. For our exuberant exploitation of scientific knowledge has begun to threaten the very life-systems that support us all. The 'laws of nature' are not as predictable as we once thought they were. Maybe they are not even 'laws' at all, for the unexpected and the unplanned can — and does — occur, undermining all our expectations.

Who would have believed that improvements in health care, leading to longer life expectancy and falling infant mortality rates, would have increased the population to the point where many of the world's nations are constantly teetering on the brink of starvation? Who would have believed that the effort to improve food production to support an increased population, spearheaded by the efficient use of pesticides and fertilizers, would have polluted the most basic human resource of all: water. Who could have foreseen that the development of modern transportation systems — whether the jet aircraft or the humble automobile — would threaten the atmosphere we all need to breathe if we are to survive? That factories making labour-saving devices would pump out noxious gases and toxic wastes? Or that in the name of 'progress' we would be killing off the very life of nature that enables us to survive as a race? Yet that is the bleak reality that faces us today and tomorrow.

In the northern hemisphere, whole forests are being devastated by the effects of acid rain, leading to catastrophic flooding in some regions of the Alps where the ground is no longer able to soak up the melting spring snows. South of the equator, the constant search for profits is leading to the rapid diminution of the earth's rain forests. In 1950, tropical hardwood exports to industrialized countries totalled 4.2 million cubic metres a year. By 1980 that trade had increased to 66 million cubic metres. And it is still rising, as acres of lush forest are sawn down to provide decoration for Western homes. In Brazil, whole areas are being burned to produce charcoal, to fire smelters which will produce iron predominantly for the European Community. And the story is the same on the other side of the globe. In Bangladesh and Nepal, so many trees have been cut down that there is not enough vegetation left to soak up the water from the ground. The result is an increasing frequency of catastrophic floods, as the melting snows of the Himalayas cascade down to the sea with nothing standing in their way. The destruction of tropical forests claims the equivalent of one football field every second.

Nor do we need to look far for evidence of impending catastrophe. As we move towards the end of the twentieth century, the signs of ecological doom are beginning to affect us all. Vacationers at some of the classiest Mediterranean resorts are afraid to go for a swim because the beaches are so polluted. The United States has suffered from dry hot summers that have decimated cattle and brought a drastic reduction of the country's grain harvest. Hurricanes of previously unknown ferocity have swept through the Caribbean. And the frightening power of earthquakes and eruptions has been felt in many places, sometimes with devastating effect.

We have terrified ourselves with our own cleverness. Parents are condemned to care for children born with previously unheard-of deformities, with more than a suspicion that it has something to do with pollution. Chernobyl is a word that strikes terror into the hearts of many people in the centre of Europe. But we now know that even this catastrophe was not unique. Increased access to classified information only serves to fuel our justifiable concerns, as we discover that in the 1950s unprotected military personnel were exposed to horrific levels of radiation, while back home in small-town America the operators of nuclear reactors scattered radioactive materials indiscriminately over the countryside. Today we are even scared to dispose of our own garbage. At this very moment shiploads of the stuff are circling the world's oceans, in the desperate search for somewhere to dump materials that no one wants and few know how to handle.

Our world is in a mess. And that's official. Referring to 1988, *Time* magazine reported: 'This year the earth spoke, like God warning Noah of the deluge. Its message was loud and clear, and suddenly people began to listen, to ponder what portents the message held.'

If the physical environment is under duress, then spare a thought for the human community. In the United States, gunfire is the eleventh most frequent cause of death overall — sixth among people under sixty-five — and for young black men in inner cities, homicide is the leading cause of death. In 1984-85, 62,897 people died of gunshot wounds in the United States — more than the number of casualties during the entire eight years of the Vietnam

War. What happens here is repeated in urban centres around the world. In how many of our major cities would you feel safe walking in daylight, let alone after dark? In some places citizens are not safe anywhere. The murder squads of right-wing dictatorships in South America find their counterparts in the secret police networks of socialist states elsewhere. While in the 'free' democracies of the West, freedom all too often means the opportunity for lunatics to wander the streets killing and maiming at will.

And what happens in small towns all over the world is reflected in the way nations deal with one another on the international scene. Moves towards peace and disarmament by the two superpowers should not allow us to forget that each of them still has enough weaponry to annihilate all of us several times over. And we can only guess at the awesome potential of chemical weapons, nerve gases and other secrets known only to the military establishment. Great strides have been taken towards the freeing of political prisoners in the Soviet Union. But for every one released there, at least three others are held in jails in other parts of the world. 'Acceptable' exploitation is still a way of life in many societies. Slavery is not altogether a thing of the past. And even in democratic states, not all citizens enjoy the freedom to reach their full potential as mature human beings. For all the affirmative action programmes of the last decade, significant groups in the United States are still at a disadvantage. Nor does the list get any shorter. Blacks, Hispanics and women are still towards the bottom of the pile, but they are now joined by AIDS sufferers and other disabled people. The situation is fundamentally no different in Europe.

Looking for answers

Is it surprising that so many people are looking for a way out of it all? Some optimists with their heads in the clouds deny that we are in a crisis. It is certainly true that pollution is nothing new. The Roman poet Seneca was bothered by it as long ago as AD61:

As soon as I had got out of the heavy air of Rome and from the stink of the smokey chimneys thereof, which, being stirred, poured forth whatever pestilent vapours and soot they held enclosed in them, I felt an alteration of my disposition.

There is also evidence of environmental neglect in several ancient civilizations. In Old Testament times, the 'Fertile Crescent' that stretched from the rivers Tigris and Euphrates on the Persian Gulf westwards to Egypt was able to sustain very significant and powerful nations. Where is the fertile crescent today? It disappeared a long time ago. Overgrazing and deforestation led to soil erosion so serious that by the time of the great biblical empires of Assyria and Babylon, enormous resources were required just to keep the irrigation channels free of silt. Eventually nature won, the canals filled up, commerce was impossible, and political power moved westwards until the discovery of oil in modern times.

The same thing happened in the early settlement of America. To start with it was an attractive land with great fertility and clear running water. But the Founding Fathers soon changed that, and by 1800 most of the land near the coast of Massachusetts was virtually useless. Industrialization only made things worse. In our own century, Pittsburgh actually took pride in being called 'the smoky city', and if a blue sky was visible that gave cause for concern. I myself lived for four years in England between the Lancashire towns of Rochdale and Oldham, and local people told me that as recently as the 1950s it had been impossible to see either town from the house where I lived — except for the two weeks in the year when the cotton mills were closed for their summer vacation!

Who is to blame for all this? 'Them', of course: politicians, scientists, capitalists, industrialists, and other pursuers of the fast buck. Conservationists have not always helped either. As long ago as 1909 the American president Theodore Roosevelt called an international conference to look at this question in relation to the northern hemisphere. But this was followed by some wild claims that discredited the legitimate concern. In 1910 one of the leading lights in this movement, Gifford Pinchot, claimed, 'We have timber for less than 30 years, anthracite coal for about 50 years . . . supplies of iron ore, minerals, oil and natural gas are being rapidly depleted.' The fact that he was so obviously mistaken did nothing to encourage people to take the business seriously.

In the second half of the twentieth century, however, there has been a growing feeling in the West that the fault should really be laid at the door of our whole cultural heritage. 'No man is an island, entire of itself . . . ' wrote the seventeenth-century English poet John Donne. We are all to some extent captives to our past, as well as being inextricably caught up by the values of our present social context. The rationalist heritage of the Enlightenment has left us with little hope of escape. 'You're on your own now' was the self-confident message of eighteenth-century philosophers and scientists. And that is exactly the message that scares the wits out of many of today's thinking people. Our own brains seem to have got us into the present mess. So what hope is there of extricating ourselves from it?

No wonder that so many are looking for renewed hope from a spiritual and supernatural direction. Are there extra-terrestrials out there, of superior intelligence to ourselves, who can help us now? Have the signposts to life's true meaning been there all along, in the remarkable remains of ancient Inca civilizations high up in the Andes, or the pyramids in Egypt? Or are they even more immediate than that — in the very stuff beneath our feet? Is the earth itself perhaps an embodiment of the divine spirit, sending us messages through the medium of natural disasters? If Western culture has provoked this state of terminal decay, what can be learned from the traditional wisdom of other nations and their religions?

These questions may seem to take us well beyond our original starting-point, which (you may remember) was the Bible. But in reality, they direct our attention to the most crucial questions of all about this remarkable book. It is all very well to claim that we should take it seriously, and to argue that it can stand up to examination on matters of textual integrity, historical authenticity, and so on. I hope that the preceding chapters have at least convinced us that it should not be dumped out of hand. But only a minority of people are interested in ancient history and related topics. Moreover, Christian believers can sometimes be far too clever for their own good — using the tools of a discredited rationalism to convince themselves that the Bible is 'true' just because it happens to fit the context of its own time, and presents a fair account of events and persons whom it describes. There is a trendy move among some contemporary Christians to try to 'prove' the truth of the Bible in this way. Any shred of evidence that seems to support it is eagerly seized upon.

Bizarre stories of the discovery of planks from Noah's ark rub shoulders with more established mythology like the Turin Shroud, while archaeological finds that do not fit the mould quite so easily are conveniently ignored. But there is more at stake than that. The Bible's ultimate message is not about history: it is about God. Even supposing we could 'prove' that the Bible's historical record is 'correct' down to every last detail, that would not — and could not — prove the essential truth of what it says about God and the meaning of human destiny. If the Bible has anything to say about life's ultimate meaning, then it needs to be judged in terms of its spiritual power and its capacity to help people cope with the everyday challenges which confront them.

The very first pages of the book of Genesis indicate that the Bible at least starts its analysis of the human predicament in the right place. The simple story of its opening chapter reflects the sort of world we would all like to believe in. A world in which plants, animals and people coexist in peaceful harmony. Where the careful ecological balance of nature operates to near perfection, and where everything is so obviously good and wholesome that we hardly need the narrative to repeat it quite so many times. Exploitation is a word that has not yet entered the vocabulary of the human race. The cosmos is under control, because it is in the hands of its loving divine Creator and Sustainer. Everybody and everything occupies their God-appointed place in this idyllic scene where each part of the cosmos can function as it was intended, and reach its own full potential in the process. The world of all our dreams. The world as it once was, perhaps. The world as we would like to see it again.

Then suddenly into this world comes the possibility of disaster. The human couple living in this garden of perfect ecological balance and personal spiritual openness have a choice to make. Could they perhaps improve on things if they took matters into their own hands? Is it actually necessary for them to live in harmony with nature, and in dependence on the God who stands behind it all? Could human reason not make a better job of things? Is there a God anyway — or could they not be their own guiding lights? And so they take that first fateful step towards chaos.

They go it alone. And what happens? Instead of continuing to enjoy a harmonious balance with their own environment, things begin to go wrong. The Garden of Eden is gone for ever. They have two sons, Cain and Abel — and in a short time their family is torn apart by selfishness and pride as Cain murders his brother. The mayhem intensifies as the love of family loyalties gives way to the law of the jungle. The chilling song of Lamech in Genesis chapter 4 says it all: 'I have killed a young man because he struck me . . . seventy-seven lives will be taken if anyone kills me.' It is not long before somebody tries to breed a super-race to take over the planet — see Genesis chapter 6. And in spite of a fairly hefty reminder of their own vulnerability — the flood! — still human self-confidence knows no limits, as ancient strategists get together to make a name for themselves by building the tower of Babel, the story of which is told in Genesis chapter 11.

We must not allow ourselves to be sidetracked into arguing about how this story can be integrated with 'scientific' explanations of the origins of things. To do so would be to lull ourselves into a false sense of security in our own wisdom, while missing the striking message that is contained here. Human self-sufficiency, self-confidence, and self-indulgence leads to disaster. No modern thinker could improve on this ancient story as a comment on the last 300 years of Western history. The tragedy is that it was there all along, and in our so-called wisdom we were too blind to see it.

Sharing out guilt

Worse than that. Many of those who did see it have actually contributed to the mess we now find ourselves in. For the Enlightenment is not the only ideological force that has helped shape the world we know today. The Judeo-Christian tradition has also played a powerful role in determining the attitudes and values of Western culture. It is therefore not surprising that Christianity in particular has come under increasingly fierce attack as a major contributing factor — if not *the* cause — of our present dilemma. It certainly does no harm to understand that Christians must shoulder much of the blame for what is happening in our world. Not by themselves, of course, for materialist atheism has done no better. Soviet scientists have pursued the quest for nuclear dominance with just as much ardour as their Western Christian counterparts, and the seas and forests of the Baltic are no less polluted than the waters of the Mediterranean — while the hand-to-mouth existence of Soviet citizens can hardly be described in terms of self-fulfilment. But there is a case for Christians to answer.

As long ago as 1967, in an article in *Science* magazine, Lynn White Jr of the University of California, Berkeley, had this to say about the historical roots of our ecological crisis:

Christianity in absolute contrast to ancient paganism and Asia's religons . . . not only established a dualism of man and nature but also insisted that it is God's will that man exploit nature for his proper ends . . . By destroying pagan animism Christianity made it possible to exploit nature with a mood of indifference to the feelings of natural objects . . . Somewhat over a century ago science and technology joined to give man powers which to judge by many of the ecological effects are out of control. If so, Christianity bears a huge burden of guilt . . . We shall continue to have a worsening ecological crisis until we reject the Christian axiom that nature has no reason for existence except to serve man.

More than twenty years on, the sexist language sounds dated. But the basic allegation is still there. There is enough truth in some of it for the charges to stick. It is undeniable that the leaders of the Industrial Revolution were all Christians, mostly motivated not only by the Calvinist work ethic but also by the conviction that the God whom they worshipped had put the world and its resources at their disposal. The way they understood this frequently brought them into conflict with other aspects of their own Christian heritage. They generally did not hesitate to regard their poorer neighbours as part of the resources to be exploited, but — with some notable exceptions — they either ignored or were blind to the contradiction between this and certain key elements in the teaching of Jesus. Like everyone else of their day, they had been deeply influenced by the Enlightenment, with its impetuous optimism about human potential. But where did this self-interested individualism nourish its roots? To a large extent, in the Protestant Reformation. Whatever they may say, Christians have been responsible for many of the world's misfortunes. The appropriate Christian response to our present plight is not to turn to self-justification, trying to rewrite the history books so that somebody else turns out to be the bad guy. Christians should be big enough to admit their mistakes, to repent of the past and commit themselves to a more humane future.

But I would want to add that a more humane future will also be — in the truest sense of the word — a more deeply Christian future. For notwithstanding the bold words quoted above from Lynn White Jr, it is not only Western Christians who must share the blame for the present crisis. Many Westerners, disenchanted with where their own culture has brought them, are now desperately searching for spiritual meaning through Eastern mysticism of various kinds. This is understandable, for one of the main goals of the traditional religions of the East has been that people should achieve some kind of harmony with the forces of nature in the plant and animal kingdom.

However, when we examine their actual performance, they cannot reasonably claim to have done better than the Christian West. The Indian subcontinent is a striking model for what an alternative world-view can achieve. And what do we find there? In spite of much piety, there is little evidence that the land and its people have fared better. Even the peace-loving Buddhists have been party to some of the most ferocious conflicts ever witnessed. Talk of oneness with the forces of the cosmos does not seem to lead to personal fulfilment for the vast majority of people. In India, where a rat is of the same cosmic significance as a child, rodents devour as much as 25 per cent of the crops while children starve. If this is living in harmony with nature, then the price is too high for most of us to pay.

In these complex issues a simple analysis can be, at best, misleading and, at worst, mischievous. This is the case with the argument about Christians and the environment. For not all Christians have assumed that nature is there for our piecemeal exploitation. The seventeenth-century English hymn-writer Isaac Watts penned the following lines, which clearly imply that animals have the right to a good life within their own community:

Let dogs delight to bark and bite,
For God hath made them so;
Let bears and lions growl and fight,
For 'tis their nature too.

Nor — contrary to popular misconception — does the Bible encourage the abuse of the natural world and its resources. For one thing, nowhere does it suggest that the world belongs to us. It always insists that it belongs to God. 'The world and all that is in it belong to the Lord; the earth and all who live on it are his,' proclaimed one of the Old Testament poets. Jesus himself said the same to his followers. God 'makes his sun shine . . . and gives rain', at the same time as he takes care of the birds and 'clothes the wild grass'. The whole Bible shows God as the caring Creator, with the land, the plants, the animals, the air, the water — and people — all dependent on him. Women and men are given the privilege of acting as God's agents, to care for the world on his behalf. 'Heaven belongs to the Lord alone,' declares Psalm 115, 'but he gave the earth to the people.' People do not own it — still less are they given the right to exploit it. When Christians claim — as they do — that the creation story in Genesis gives them authority to play God with the world, they are motivated more by the concern to maximize profits than to discover the true meaning of their faith.

Human exploitation

The crisis now facing the earth is just the most extreme example of the in-built human propensity to selfishness. Our exploitation of the natural environment is rivalled in enormity only by our capacity for ripping off other members of the human species. Here again, Christians are not blameless though the Bible is, if anything, even more outspoken on this point. Hardly surprising when you consider that one of its central events — the exodus — tells how God stepped in to release hard-pressed slaves from the imperialistic grip of a self-confessed dictator, and delivered them into their own land.

Yet recent history again shows that Christians have often been distinctly lukewarm towards the Bible's position on such matters. Who initiated and for generations sustained the enslavement of black people in the southern states of America? White Christians, of course. Christians whose commitment to their own religion motivated them to share it with their slaves. Sunday by Sunday, therefore, they were taken along to church to be told that though things were pretty bad for them here and now, there was always the possibility of an improvement in circumstances once this life was over — if they served their masters faithfully!

The same kind of thinking is still embraced by some Christians today. South Africa is arguably one of the most religious nations in the world. It is also one of the most despised, because of its policy of separate development for the various races: the doctrine of apartheid. Most people think of apartheid as a political theory. Some want to compare it with Hitler's demonic dream of a pure Aryan race that would subjugate the world. But its origins and sustaining ideology are religious. Originally promulgated as theological dogma by the fiercely Calvinistic Dutch Reformed Church back in 1857, apartheid was gradually adopted as a political doctrine in the course of the twentieth century. As recently as 1974 a report of the Dutch Reformed Church claimed that 'the Scriptures . . . teach and uphold the ethnic diversity of the human race . . . a political system based on the autogenous or separate development of various population groups can be justified from the Bible.'

Here again, there have always been Christians who realized that the message of Jesus Christ cannot be reconciled with this kind of thinking. One of the most striking U-turns of modern times came in October 1986, when the Dutch Reformed Church in South Africa reversed its position, and admitted that 'the application of apartheid as a political and social system which injures people and unjustly benefits one group above another cannot be accepted on Christian ethical grounds since it conflicts with the principle of neighbourly love and righteousness'. Others had known this for some time, and if white South African Christians had been open to learn from the experience of others, they could possibly have averted the bloodshed and misery which has so sadly devastated their beautiful country for the past quarter of a century and more.

As long ago as 1688 a Quaker Monthly Meeting near Philadelphia had considered a resolution deploring slavery — though it was to take a further seventy years before the Philadelphia yearly meeting could be persuaded to outlaw slave-trading and slave-holding by Quakers. American Methodists also have an honourable anti-slavery record. In 1780 the Baltimore Methodist Conference demanded that its travelling preachers should set free the slaves which some of them kept. Their official resolution declared that 'slave-keeping is contrary to the laws of God, man and nature, and hurtful to society, contrary to the dictates of conscience and pure religion...' Meanwhile, back in Europe it was the Christian activist William Wilberforce who eventually succeeded in persuading the British parliament to abolish slavery in its empire in 1833. Yet even in the twentieth century the debate still rumbles on. When Martin Luther King Jr wanted to claim his full citizenship rights he was assassinated. There are still white preachers around who claim that their Christian God is a racist. 'I can cite passages that will curdle your blood,' threatens American revivalist preacher the Rev. Charles Conley Lynch, Bible in hand: 'There is no other book that presents more violence in defence of racial purity.'

Which are these passages? Genesis chapter 9 verses 18 to 27 has been used for years by white racists to 'prove' that black people are cursed by God. We need not ponder the details of the story, except to notice that in it Noah places a curse on 'Canaan'. How then do you move from that to the assertion that whites are better than blacks? With great difficulty, and a lot of theological wire-pulling.

For the fact is that the Bible is not a racist book at all. The very next chapter of Genesis actually praises several people who are categorically identified there as the ancestors of black nations. And though the Old Testament is essentially the story of just one nation, there is a strong emphasis everywhere on that nation serving as a source of blessing for all the nations, for instance in Genesis chapter 12 verse 3. We have already referred to the story of Genesis chapter 1, which describes people, without any racial or other qualification, as being made in God's image.

In the New Testament, a non-white person — Jesus — occupies centre stage. That in itself is a powerful statement about the Christian message. Hollywood movies that always portray him as a white Anglo-Saxon Protestant cannot alter the obvious facts of history. Nor are we surprised to discover that whenever Jesus encounters discrimination of any sort — racism included — he clearly dissociated himself from it. Paul fought tooth and nail to oppose the idea that the church should be anything less than multiracial. Even though it was his own people — Jewish Christians — who wanted to restrict membership to their own kind, he had no hesitation in standing up to them. And it was from his pen that we have these words: 'there is no difference between Jews and Gentiles, between slaves and free men . . . you are all one in union with Christ Jesus.' They are found in chapter 3 of his letter to the Galatians.

Physical enslavement is not the only way to exercise power over the lives of other people. It is the most visible, perhaps, in that the exploited classes are there for all to see. But there are more insidious forms of the same malady around today. Much of the Two-Thirds World has been condemned to a life of economic slavery to Western bankers and governments for the indefinite future. Here again, so-called 'Christian' nations have loaned vast amounts of money to the poorer peoples of the world. Mostly to enable them to purchase the products of Western technology, some of which they do not need anyway. As a result, the world is rapidly sinking under a great tidal wave of debt, with some countries having little chance of ever being able to repay what they owe. Many — like Brazil — have no natural resources other than the tropical rain forests. So they cut the trees down in a desperate struggle to meet their liabilities, and in the process simply add to the total global predicament. Concern for the environment cannot easily be divorced from care for the world's people.

The Bible also has some interesting things to say about this. For it is not only the physical world that belongs to God, but its material resources as well. When Israel found new life in their own land, it was given to the whole nation — not to selected individuals. For practical purposes individuals had their own plot, but strict rules were laid down to ensure that the title deeds could not be sold for personal gain. There was no such thing as exclusive personal ownership of land. At best, an individual might lease a piece of property, since in the 'Year of Jubilee' it would be returned to its original owner. Time and again the Old Testament affirms that God has a special concern for those who are poor, destitute, and marginalized. This conviction was so central that it found a natural place in the music and poetry of the nation. 'The Lord . . . lifts the poor from the dust and raises the needy from their misery,' sang Hannah the mother of Samuel. Nor was this mere romantic sentiment. The prophets, guardians of the nation's faith and moral values, were outspoken in their condemnation of those who tried to get rich on the backs of the poor and disadvantaged. Even the king himself came to grief when he tried to seize property from one of his subjects(see 1 Kings chapter 21 for the details).

The same note sounds throughout the message of Jesus. It is more than coincidence that in all his parables, it is the rich and prosperous who are the villains, and the marginalized who are the heroes. At the very outset of his teaching, Jesus declared (quoting the Old Testament) that 'The Spirit of the Lord is upon me, because he has chosen me to bring good news to the poor. He has sent me to proclaim liberty to the captives . . . to set free the oppressed . . . ' — words found in Luke chapter 4. There is only one thing that is 'good news' for the poor, and that is the amelioration of their plight. That concern is central to the Christian message as contained in the Bible.

Equality

Not all discrimination is visible. Or so many feminists would tell us. And they are right. Here again, Christians do not have a particularly impressive record. One of the more unsavoury spectacles of recent times has been the sight of various churches debating whether women should be admitted to the ranks of the clergy. For me the crucial question is not whether women should be ordained to the ministry as presently defined by men, but whether that concept and style of ministry actually reflects the demands of the message of Christ, for either women or men. By any reckoning, the style of ministry men have evolved for themselves down the centuries has not been one of the church's major success stories. Perhaps again because it generally reflects a different concept of church from what can most easily be found in the Bible. Why, I ask myself, should far-sighted and gifted women wish to ape inadequate procedures formulated by men, instead of developing their own distinctive — and potentially more valuable — insights into the nature of the Christian message? That question has been largely ignored, at least in the public debates. Having said that, however, it is obvious that much of the resistance to fuller participation by women is sheer prejudice. Where is the logic in the claim that because Jesus was male he cannot be properly represented by a female? And when leading male clerics make the grotesque claim that a woman's menstrual cycle somehow disqualifies her from dispensing the Eucharist, do they really expect to be taken seriously? Genuine arguments about theology are one thing, but primitive superstition of this kind is something else altogether.

The church has a lot to answer for here, as elsewhere. But again, notice that Christians have generally been no worse than anyone else. Long before the time of Jesus, the Greek philosopher Aristotle described a female as 'a kind of mutilated male', by which he meant that 'Females are imperfect males, accidentally created by the father's inadequacy or by the malign influence of a moist south wind'. Josephus, the Jewish writer whom we met in a previous chapter, had a similar opinion. 'The woman', he wrote, 'is inferior to the man in every way'. Jewish men thanked the Almighty every morning because they had not been made either Gentiles, or slaves, or women. And the Quran comments: 'Men have authority over women because Allah has made the one superior to the other . . . those from whom you fear disobedience, admonish them and send them to beds apart and beat them . . . ' Even the generally progressive Gandhi has this to say about Indian habits: 'A Hindu husband regards himself as lord and master of his wife, who must ever dance attendance upon him.'

Many people have the impression that the Bible, if not the actual source of discrimination, does nothing to present a different point of view. Nothing could be further from the truth. The Bible was of course written in a patriarchal society and naturally makes reference to the assumptions held in such a culture. But it also contains within itself the seeds of the destruction of any theory of male dominance. From start to finish its message affirms the intrinsic worth of women, and implies their rights as equal partners with men. Take the story of creation in Genesis chapter 1. It tells how God created man, as the final crowning glory of his work. Or does it? Read more carefully: 'God said, "And now we will make human beings; they will be like us and resemble us . . . ". So God created human beings, making them to be like himself. He created them male and female, blessed them . . . ' We must not allow ourselves to be misinformed by the familiar and traditional language of English Bibles. Despite generations of sexist translations, that is what the original Hebrew text actually says. Now what does it mean? First, that man and woman are equal: both are made in God's image. And second, that both of them together share in care of God's world, in which they live. Equal in status and equal in function and responsibility.

Some feminists argue that the story in Genesis chapter 2 is of a different character. Here we have the story of how a woman was made from a rib taken from the side of the first man. Does this imply some kind of male superiority, especially in view of the fact that she is made because the man can find no 'suitable companion' among the animals? Is it not saying that before a woman can have meaning, there needs to be a man?

If the book of Genesis had been written by modern rationalist scientists, no doubt that would be a possible conclusion to draw. But when we read poetry, people of sensitivity usually have no hesitation in acknowledging that words can be used to convey profound truths quite independently of their literal meaning. When the Scottish poet Robert Burns composed a song for his lover, he described her as 'a red, red rose all newly sprung in June'. Only a half-wit would conclude he was in love with a flower. Similarly, I find it impossible to imagine that the Genesis story is claiming that women are in any way inferior to men. It is saying that women take their place in the order of things *alongside* men. To be a whole person, the man needs a woman — and vice versa. Neither man nor woman is defective because of that: each of them has the potential for personal self-fulfilment that can only be achieved through interaction with another person. Peter Lombard, a twelfth-century bishop of Paris, grasped the point when he wrote of this passage: 'Eve was not taken from the feet of Adam to be his slave, nor from his head to be his lord, but from his side to be his partner.' And partnership for the Bible means exactly what it means for us today.

But, you may ask, is God not always male in the Bible? Wrong again. The God of the Bible is of course fundamentally indescribable. God cannot be defined analytically, as it were, by reference to what he is made of, but only by analogy to persons and experiences with which we are familiar from other areas of human life. God can be described as a Father, because his relationship to people can be as close and life-giving as the best of human family ties. But God is also the mother of her people. In an early piece of poetry, the 'Song of Moses' in Deuteronomy chapter 32, we find this statement: 'You deserted the Rock, who fathered you; you forgot the God who gave you birth.' God is the divine parent — male and female. Elsewhere in the Old Testament, God cries out 'like a woman in labour' in Isaiah chapter 42, and showers her people with the affection of a mother in Isaiah chapter 49 verse 15 and chapter 66 verse 13. Psalm 131 compares God's love with quiet rest in the arms of a divine mother. Jesus too uses female imagery to describe his own love for people (in Matthew chapter 23 verse 37). When you remember that all this was written in an ancient male-dominated culture, and that the major challenge to Israel's faith came from a religion which gave a high profile to sexual worship of the female form, then the acceptance of female imagery with which to describe God is all the more striking.

However, there is a consistency here with other Old Testament statements about the relationship of women and men. If, as the creation story in Genesis affirms, both are made in the image of God, then that would most naturally imply that there is some aspect of God's own being that corresponds to the feminine as well as the masculine.

When we come to the New Testament, the affirmation of woman is even more far-reaching. Jesus is clearly portrayed as divine. Yet he comes into our world not through the agency of a man, but specifically and exclusively as the son of a woman, Mary. Throughout the course of his life he showed no reticence in overturning conventional Jewish practices relating to women. It was against the Law for a Jewish man to talk to a woman in public — even his wife, sister, or daughter. Jesus not only did this, but actually shared his teaching with them as well. The fact that no woman is listed among the twelve disciples is immaterial, for the witness of women played a significant part in his life. They were even the primary witnesses to the resurrection. This implied equality of women and men continued in the life of the early church. In Acts chapter 1, women are specifically mentioned as part of the group of church leaders in Jerusalem, and on the Day of Pentecost they are singled out for specific mention as the recipients, along with men, of the Holy Spirit.

Paul, of course, is another matter — and a subject too complex to cover at great length here. For a long time, he has been the fall-guy of women's libbers. But it is not so simple. Far from being the archetypal male chauvinist he is made out to be, Paul was perfectly happy to work alongside women, some of whom were close friends. His most extensive list of greetings to Christian leaders in Romans chapter 16 includes many women, to one of whom he gives the title 'apostle'. This reference has been surreptitiously obscured by male Bible translators, who habitually refer to the two people mentioned in Romans chapter 16 verse 7 as 'men of note among the apostles'. But of the two names given — Andronicus and Junias — only the first is a man's name, and the most natural reading is to suppose they were a husband and wife partnership, and both were 'apostles'.

In any case, it was Paul who penned those words to which we have already referred in connection with slavery. 'There is no difference,' he wrote in Galatians chapter 3, 'between slaves and free men, between men and women.' Whatever else he may say, we cannot ignore or play down that declaration of the principle of equality. In point of fact, a proper understanding of the allegedly chauvinistic passages in 1 Corinthians chapters 11 and 14 soon shows that they are actually an extension of his stated practice of freedom and equality, not a restriction of it. Modern detractors of Paul usually choose to refer only to what he says about women in those chapters, but in each of them he also tells men quite firmly that on occasion it would be better if they kept quiet in church too. To deal with awkward men and cantankerous women in the same breath, and to give similar advice to each, is to assume they are equal, not the opposite. When properly understood, Paul has a good claim to be not the villain, but the patron saint of women's lib!

Expanding horizons

Christianity is growing rapidly today all over the world. Already more than 1.6 billion people claim to follow Jesus Christ, and the number is increasing all the time. According to the massively researched *World Christian Encyclopedia*, in sub-Saharan Africa alone, over 16,000 people become Christians every day! In some places, notably South America and south-east Asia, the growth rate of the Christian church has actually outstripped the growth rate of the overall population. People are becoming Christians faster than they are becoming Marxists, or Muslims, or anything else, and the church has a sound claim to be the fastest-growing mass movement in the world today. The surprising thing is that at the same time, the church is declining in Western Europe and North America. The same source reveals that every day in northern Europe, some 7,500 people leave the church. In the last fifty years, there has been a significant shift in Christianity's centre of gravity — away from the white Western nations and towards the developing peoples of the rest of the world. Women and men of all races are discovering that the message of Jesus Christ has great relevance to life in a changing world scene.

Significantly, the Bible is at the heart of this quiet religious revolution. With growing literacy, more and more people are able to read it for themselves. As they do, they are finding in its pages a message that is far more radical and relevant than they ever thought possible. In the last twenty years, the face of Latin America has been changed beyond recognition as ordinary people have been inspired and challenged by what they hear the Bible saying. Even people with no declared interest in current affairs can hardly miss the fact that something is happening here — and in South Africa and other places — and much of it is connected with Christians and the church. Oscar Romero, archbishop of San Salvador, became a modern martyr when he was gunned down in his cathedral. Desmond Tutu, Anglican archbishop in South Africa, is a familiar face on our television screens. But for every one like them there are hundreds of ordinary people whose lives have been radically changed as a result of their rediscovery of the message of the Bible.

As simple people meet to read and pray in small groups throughout the Two-Thirds World, a change is taking place in their perception of the message of Jesus Christ. They can see well enough that white Christians often confused Christian missions with Western imperialism. They recognize that the Bible's message has been misunderstood, and sometimes quite deliberately so. But they can also see that when it is stripped of centuries of ecclesiastical tradition, it contains a vital message for our times. More than that: it holds out the only real hope for our future. No one can yet predict what will be the ultimate outcome of this movement. But in global terms it may well prove to be one of the great turning-points of human history — at least as important as the Reformation and the European Enlightenment.

Already many of the sacred cows of conventional Christianity are being sacrificed. Take a very basic question: what is the church? For many Westerners it is a distinctive building, a familiar sight in all our towns and cities. Others see it as a rich and prosperous business empire — part of the worn-out systems of the world that seem so powerless to do anything really fundamental to give new meaning to life. But the Bible paints a rather different picture. The real church is not buildings — still less institutions — but people.

To understand this, we need to step back and listen afresh to the words of Jesus and Paul. Jesus' message was simple. 'The time has come,' he announced, 'God's Kingdom is here. Turn your life around, and believe in this good news.' These words are found in Mark chapter 1. In stories and through actions Jesus declared that from now on, things could be different. The unacceptable could find new acceptance. The outcasts could be welcomed in, the wounded could be healed, and the spiritual searchers could find true enlightenment. Women and men, children too — indeed the whole creation — could find the peace and harmony which has eluded the cosmos for so long. Unlike later Christians, Jesus never describes God's kingdom exclusively as a promise of better things to come in the future. He was the king, he declared, and things could be different here and now.

In his own relationships with others, he constantly spoke about the way God's power could break down barriers. The earliest disciples in Jerusalem did the same. The vocation of their community was to be God's kingdom in miniature. To be a follower of Jesus was to be a part of an alternative society. A society based not on selfishness, greed and exploitation, but on the new freedom announced by Jesus: freedom to love God, and to love and serve others. The book of Acts reveals that instead of amassing wealth either for individuals or for the institution, 'they would sell their property and possessions, and distribute the money among all, according to what each one needed. Day after day they met as a group . . . and they had their meals together in their homes . . . praising God . . . and every day the Lord added to their group . . .'

Is it any wonder that the early church enjoyed such a phenomenal growth rate? They offered a plausible alternative way of life, that had the power to fulfil the deepest aspirations of the human spirit. People of diverse social, racial and religious backgrounds were bound together by the ties of a new and radical friendship. Because of their commitment to Jesus Christ, they discovered a new level of commitment to others. Their whole value system was totally transformed, and when people asked for proof that God had the power to change things, they needed to look no further than the church.

These primitive communities were more than just a new social structure. Far more. The church was not a human institution: it was the supernatural work of God. When a group of disheartened and disillusioned followers of Jesus became a strong and courageous band, it was not because they had applied some special technique of meditation, hypnosis, or creative visualization. Life took on new meaning when they realized that they needed God's power to change them, and that personal transformation was a gift made available by Jesus Christ to anyone who would accept it. It was not easy to admit their own flaws and weaknesses. But when the power of the Holy Spirit flooded into their lives, they knew that at last they had made contact with the ultimate power behind the cosmos. The church was not something they dreamed up for themselves. It did not belong to its leaders — not even to the apostles. It belonged to the Lord, Jesus himself, and within it those who trusted him found new life and fresh meaning.

This was the vision that inspired Paul, the one-time Pharisee, to share the life-changing message with communities all over the Roman Empire. He was not interested in winning converts to some ecclesiastical cause. He gave all he had that others might share his own experience of total release and self-fulfilment through the work of God's supernatural Spirit in his life.

Personal transformation is only one aspect of the Christian message. Paul was certain that it also produced a new form of human community. What he says about this in 1 Corinthians chapter 12 is so distinctive that it is worth including it all here:

Christ is like a single body, which has many parts; it is still one body, even though it is made up of different parts. In the same way, all of us, whether Jews or Gentiles, whether slaves or free, have been baptized into the one body by the same Spirit, and we have all been given the one Spirit to drink. For the body itself is not made up of only one part, but of many parts. If the foot were to say, 'Because I am not a hand, I don't belong to the body', that would not keep it from being a part of the body. And if the ear were to say, 'Because I am not an eye, I don't belong to the body', that would not keep it from being a part of the body. If the whole body were just an eye, how could it hear? And if it were only an ear, how could it smell? As it is, however, God put every different part in the body just as he wanted it to be. There would not be a body if it were all only one part! As it is, there are many parts but one body.

So then, the eye cannot say to the hand, 'I don't need you!' Nor can the head say to the feet, 'Well, I don't need you!' On the contrary, we cannot do without the parts of the body that seem to be weaker; and those parts that we think aren't worth very much are the ones which we treat with greater care ... If one part of the body suffers, all the other parts suffer with it; if one part is praised, all the other parts share its happiness.

All of you are Christ's body, and each one is a part of it ...

For people whose experience of the church is limited to the traditional formal structures of historic Western Christianity, this is indeed a radical concept. Paul takes his start from the physiology of the ancient world. But it is not difficult to see what he is saying. He thinks of the human body as a complex piece of machinery, with parts of different size, shape and constitution, all required to work together in various locations and in different ways to ensure the smooth operation of the whole body. A body without an ear or an eye would be impaired — just as would a body with no hands or feet. To ask whether a hand is more attractive than an eye is an absurd question for both are required as they are if the human body is to work properly.

The unity within diversity that is the key to physical health is also a fundamental requirement, he suggests, for spiritual health in the human community. Individual people can be compared to ears, hands, feet, or whatever. No two individuals are identical. But in the renewed community which is Christ's church everyone can discover their own unique significance as persons, while being caught up into a spiritual reality greater than the sum of the individual parts. Paul goes on to describe what this would mean in practical terms. When Christians meet together for worship or companionship, he says, everyone has something to offer to the corporate life of the whole body. Through this others can be enriched, and our own personal value can be affirmed.

This is the exact opposite of what traditionally happens in most churches. Ecclesiastical structures generally allow full participation by only a minority. Debates about whether women should be accepted as clergy only conceal the fact that the majority of the church's people — women and men — are silent spectators of rituals carried out exclusively by the leadership. If Paul could return today, he would be appalled at the way the church has been hijacked by self-opinionated religious experts concerned more with the efficient maintenance of ecclesiastical bureaucracy than with enabling ordinary people to meet God. It never occurred to him that Christians would be so brainwashed by the individualism bred into us through the influence of Reformation and Enlightenment as to imagine that priests and other religious functionaries could have a monopoly on the gifts of God's Spirit. On the Day of Pentecost, the power of God had been poured out on all Christ's people, thereby abolishing all the barriers of spoiled human society. That is why Paul was so uncompromising in his certainty that the divisions of sex, race, and social class were now broken down by the message of Christ.

Far from being the establishment figure that he is often made out to be, Paul was a radical visionary to his very fingertips. He has been misunderstood and maligned for too long by people who have selectively majored on those bits of his message that could be used to support their own cosy thinking, while ignoring the rest.

In the light of the experiences of the introverted Martin Luther and the egocentric rationalism of the Enlightenment it could seem plausible to interpret Paul's understanding of salvation exclusively in terms of freedom from personal guilt, while missing his crucial insistence that true spiritual freedom runs far deeper. It includes everything that would inhibit the development of the human personality to reach its full potential and become what God intended us to be. It also has a place for the renewal of the physical world, which is waiting to be set free as well as Romans chapter 8 verses 18 to 23 reveals. To be set free by Christ means being released into a new world in which we can find our own true identity, relating to each other in free and open friendship because God has taken the initiative in freely sharing his own love with our world through Christ.

The rediscovery of this striking message has breathed new vitality into the Christian church all over the world. So what is the church, according to the Bible? This is how the South American theologian Gustavo Gutierrez puts it:

The gospel summons into being a people's church. A church which springs up from the people . . . we are called to build the church from below, from the poor, from the situation of the exploited classes, the excluded races, and the despised cultures.

Once released from the cultural bias of the traditional Western mind-set, the Bible is strikingly relevant to the needs of today's people. Foremost among them is the universal desire for true human community. Cultures in many parts of the world easily acknowledge that none of us exists by ourselves. This is also a basic contention of the Bible's message. In the Old Testament, Psalm 68 declares that 'God sets the lonely in families', and throughout the writings of the prophets it is emphasised that faith in God is not a personal and private affair, but must affect the way we behave in relation to other people. Worship itself is depicted as a vehicle for the spread of God's love throughout the community (see for example Amos chapter 5 verses 21 to 24 and Micah chapter 6 verses 6 to 8). And Jesus reinforced all this in his own teaching about the nature of true discipleship. 'Love God,' he said in Matthew chapter 22 — but then he added, as a second fundamental proposition, not an afterthought, 'and love your neighbour as yourself.' The resolution of the disharmony we see all around us today is not an optional extra, but is part and parcel of any true devotion to the God of the Bible.

From this perspective, the Bible's message is surprisingly relevant to our present needs. Take the story of the exodus of the Israelites from Egypt found in the book of Exodus, for example. Traditional Christian understanding of this has focused on two points. On the one hand there has been extensive discussion as to whether it all took place. What would modern scientists have seen had they been there? How much can we allow to filter through the sieve of our enlightened rationalistic minds? Others, afraid of asking such questions, look instead for hidden meanings in it all. Perhaps the exodus is some kind of allegorical picture of what it means to be a Christian? That way, the blood on the doorposts of the houses becomes a symbol of Christ's death on the cross, and the waters of the Red Sea are an appropriate symbol for baptism. Even though there are crucial differences — not least the fact that baptism always involves somebody getting wet, whereas the whole point of the exodus was that they stayed dry!

But what happens when we discard this obsession with theoretical abstractions, and instead look at the story through the eyes of the poor and oppressed people in today's world? At once, it all starts to come alive. The story tells how a smallish band of dispirited slaves escaped from Egypt under the leadership of Moses, eventually to establish a new way of life in their own land. A group of dispossessed, exploited and disadvantaged people are rescued from the power of a totalitarian dictatorship and given their freedom — and the Bible makes the amazing claim that God has done it! It reflects his view of how things ought to be.

The same theme continues as the escaping slaves reach their new land of Canaan. Other people already lived there — organised into small city-states by powerful rulers who frequently exploited their peasants and certainly kept all the real power to themselves. Over against this, the escaped slaves had a different view, gained in their meeting with God at Mt Sinai and the Law which had been entrusted to them on that occasion. On that basis, they set about the establishment of a different regime, characterized by justice and inspired by the example of God himself.

Now think of Jesus' teaching. He frequently describes God's kingdom as a community in which people find true personal fulfilment, in which the outcasts of conventional society — people like tax gatherers, women, prostitutes, and the disabled — can be accepted. A place where disciples will love one another because they have experienced the love of God himself. For Jesus, people and their needs were of fundamental importance. They certainly took precedence over theological abstractions.

But the Bible does not stop there. Not only does it give a blueprint for human life in the renewed community of the church. It also looks forward to the restoration of harmony within nature itself. In Romans chapter 8 Paul again writes of the hope that 'creation itself will one day be set free from its slavery to decay and will share the glorious freedom of the children of God' and, in Colossians chapter 1, he affirms that the cosmos itself is one of God's primary concerns, and that through Jesus Christ the balance of nature will ultimately be restored.

9

Hope Beyond Despair

The Bible's agenda runs remarkably parallel to the spiritual search of many in the West today. It is premature to talk of the widespread disintegration of our civilization. But we have created a world so frightening that some are unable to face up to the reality of it. So how will we escape? Long ago, the writer of Ecclesiastes observed that God has 'set eternity in the hearts of men', and it is a feature of our times that people are looking for somebody or something to call 'God' in a way that we have not seen — in the West at least — for several generations. Where will we find this transcendent reality that can give meaning to life?

The gurus of modern popular religion tell us that the Bible and its message is unbelievable, that Christians around the world whose lives are being transformed by the dynamic power of the Holy Spirit are deluded and naive. But things are not quite as simple as they think. It is just as likely that we ourselves are deluded by reading the Bible in the light of our own spiritual poverty. Few of us experience the supernatural power of the living God in our own lives, and so we convince ourselves it is all a myth, telling ourselves at the same time that it is somehow more superior to be sceptics and unbelievers. But what advanced and sophisticated alternatives are being advocated in place of a simple trust in the living God? For the most part, a return to Dark Ages superstition and sheer triviality.

Listen to the answer given by bestselling psychiatrist Scott Peck in his book *The Road Less Travelled*:

If you desire wisdom greater than your own, you can find it inside you . . . To put it plainly, our unconscious is God . . . It is for the individual to become totally, wholly God.

So what's new? Remember the ancient Gnostics whom we met in a previous chapter? They thought exactly the same. And they were so convincing that they disappeared, almost without a trace. If the world's only hope is to be found in personal self-awareness, then the future is even bleaker than the past and the present. It is our own inability to make things better that has led us to search for ultimate answers in the first place. If there is no absolute reality beyond the depths of our own existence, then the whole of life is an illusion. It can have no ultimate meaning, and will only accelerate our descent into the vortex of despair. In addition, this kind of philosophy can only lead to a selfish disregard for the social and global dimensions of the problems facing us today. Writing in *Greenpeace Chronicles* for August 1979, Bob Hunter claims that such self-discovery holds the key to responsible ecological concern for our planet:

The world is Our Body . . . Mother Earth is not passive. To align oneself with Her energies is to liberate . . . the Godhead within you, to be lifted into a higher state of being.

But the logic is fundamentally flawed. Believing that we are all a part of some great cosmic 'God' will lead to a moral system in which personal achievement and personal growth is the main thing to aim for. Personal growth is now defined as the freedom to decide what we will do, and when and how we will do it — hence the increasing popularity of fantasy games and novels where readers choose for themselves what will happen next. But if this is the only guide we have for our behaviour, it will lead to disaster.

It is precisely the act of choosing for ourselves, without regard either for the welfare of others or for the cosmic consequences, that has encouraged us to spoil our planet in the first place. We have all suffered enough from social and moral irresponsibility, and sheer selfishness, without now elevating it to a virtue and calling it 'God'. People in the Western 'free' world have been conditioned to question any talk of absolutes — whether in moral options, or in the truth claims of religious beliefs. Yet we can draw a straight line from the belief that there are no absolute moral imperatives to the conclusion that no one can ultimately be responsible for their own actions. To observe that we have created our own living hell by making choices that suit our own interest groups is not dogmatism: it is simply stating an obvious fact.

Charting a safe course

Where can we chart a safe course for the future? Specifically, does the Bible have anything relevant to say? Indeed it does — as we have seen in our review of some of the great issues of the day. But its message goes broader and deeper than that. It presents a radical challenge to our thinking. It has no place for the belief that there is some great cosmic force that permeates everything, nor does it define salvation in terms of personal self-discovery. It affirms that behind it all, and above it all there stands a unique and unrivalled divine Being. This is the God with whom all things began, through whom they are sustained, and in whose power alone the key to the future is to be found.

But there is more. God is not an impersonal force, but a personal Being. A Being whose love for the totality of the world has been there from the very beginning. And whose personal concern for the cosmos and its inhabitants has been expressed in particular through the life and teaching, death and resurrection of Jesus Christ. A God whose spiritual power is freely available to those who will open their lives to the personal dynamic of the Holy Spirit.

All honest searchers after truth know that personal transformation is at the heart of any hope we may have for the future of our world. But how can there be such personal transformation without a personal God? How can we comprehend the nature of that transformation without concrete human example such as we find in Jesus? To suggest that persons can be changed by their incorporation into or awareness of some impersonal and unpredictable cosmic force is to blaspheme and undervalue our own humanity. Jesus does not offer an esoteric unity in a disembodied and dehumanized form with some ultimate cosmic process. Nor does he offer fulfilment by escaping from the harshness of life in this world. The heart of his message — indeed of the whole Bible — is in the opening paragraph of John's Gospel: 'The Word became a human being and, full of grace and truth, lived among us.'

This is a bold statement indeed. If it is true, it offers a hope beyond despair. It means there is a future for our world and its people. That life here and now can make sense as we meet God within it.

Where then will spiritual transformation come from? One popular belief is that over many generations our potential for spiritual fulfilment has been numbed by the rationalism that is endemic in our culture. We have been conditioned to think in only one way, using only one half of our brain, we are told. In right-handed people, the left brain does the thinking, the right the feeling. Our educational training has generally encouraged the left, leaving the right relatively undeveloped, and it is the right that will enable us to make contact with the force behind the cosmos. In an article in the *Los Angeles Times* for 19 August 1987, Hollywood personality Shirley Maclaine explained it this way:

A person who thinks laterally, or with the right hemisphere, is capable of seeing a broader connectedness to events that would be little more than a contradictory puzzle to a left-brained Westerner.

She went on to claim that

Eastern thinkers are more open to right-brained] intuitive thinking

and that this

addresses higher dimensions and more realities, which enable us to feel connected to the source of what I call God Energy. It speaks to the language of the soul, the universality of the spirit . . .

There is some truth in this, muddled up with a large dose of superstitious nonsense. It is of course a physiological fact that the two hemispheres of the brain generally control different functions. But not invariably. Medical research in the University of Washington has shown that almost 7 per cent of people are not built that way at all, and in others who suffer brain damage the functions normally performed in the damaged side can be taken over and performed equally well by the other. However, the general distinction is valid enough, as is the view that our predominantly rationalistic culture has encouraged us to believe that the only 'real' truth is what comes out of the left brain. As a result, many Westerners are emotionally and spiritually undeveloped.

The church itself provides ample evidence to support this general claim. 'The Word became flesh,' wrote John. Yet for the last 2,000 years, Christian theologians have spent almost all their energies trying to put it back into words again. Even among the followers of Jesus Christ, rationalism has often triumphed at the expense of spirituality. Many ordinary people are puzzled when church leaders appear to deny what Jesus seems to have affirmed, or when they question fundamental aspects of the Bible's message.

In particular, Western Christians have generally been embarrassed by any talk of the supernatural. Even those who feel obliged to defend the supernatural as an authentic part of the story of Jesus frequently adopt theological theories to give an apparently rational explanation as to why it plays no part in their own spiritual experience. As a result, those right-brained thinkers who are aware of the need for personal transformation as a mystical, spiritual process find themselves turned off by the fact that so many Christians are thorough-going rationalists. Because the church can apparently offer no meaningful and immediate contact with the spiritual world, they turn instead to messages allegedly channelled through extra-terrestrials. Because some Christians sneer at the possibility that the Holy Spirit is at work to bring healing into our lives today, genuine seekers after truth turn instead to crystals and pyramids. Yet Jesus said in John chapter 14: 'Whoever believes in me will do what I do — yes, he will do even greater things, because I am going to the Father . . . ' And the life of the earliest Christian community was characterized by the fact mentioned in Acts chapter 2 that 'many miracles and wonders were being done through the apostles, and everyone was filled with awe . . . '

It is no coincidence that alongside the growth of the world church today there is a rediscovery of the spiritual power available to Christians through the work of the Holy Spirit. Awareness of the supernatural is playing a large part in the renewal of many Christian groups in the West as well. Some traditionalists in the church are afraid of it. They dismiss this 'right-brained' faith as readily — and as unfairly — as Shirley Maclaine dismisses 'left-brained' serious thinking. But the Bible preserves a balance between the two. We are rational beings, and nothing can change that. Paul himself — who had a very extensive right-brained experience of the Spirit (see the first half of 2 Corinthians chapter 12) — advised readers of his first letter to the Thessalonians to 'put all things to the test', and in 1 Corinthians chapter 12 included both teaching and discernment among the gifts of the Spirit.

The Bible encourages us to use our God-given intellectual powers. The faith to which Jesus calls us is not irrational, nor even non-rational. It is based on facts that are open to investigation like any other facts. That is why so many chapters of this book have been taken up with historical and textual questions. And having analyzed what the facts are, we need to be prepared to act on the basis of them. If, as I believe, the facts give no credence at all to the crazy notion that the Bible is a hoax dreamed up by nasty men in the early church, then we must reject the suggestion that its message has been doctored to keep us all in spiritual darkness. If, as I also believe, the New Testament Gospels have a good claim to contain an authentic portrait of Jesus, then we must reject the claim that the 'real' Jesus is to be found in secret Gnostic Gospels. To respond to Jesus Christ requires an intellectual conversion. If Jesus Christ is all that the Bible claims, then no thinking person can afford to ignore him.

But being a disciple involves much more than just a change in the way we think. It also demands a 'right-brained' commitment of our emotions and personal being to him, and an acceptance of the values of his kingdom as the key both to personal spiritual transformation and the future of the whole cosmos. Contrary to what some in the church think, this is not a cheap or easy option. Nor is it a retreat into sentimentality or unrealistic idealism. It is not an escape route for inadequates from the hardships of life in this world. It is for people looking for a challenge that is big enough to be worth committing themselves to. When Jesus stood before his first disciples, he spoke simply and directly. 'Take up your cross,' he said, 'and follow me.'

Start where you are, bring what you have. Take up the mess that you have made of the world. Bring the muddle of your own spiritual darkness. Lift up the spiritual alienation that you have created for yourself through sheer arrogance as you have tried to put yourself in the place of God. Take it up, said Jesus, and let me deal with it all. He offered nothing less than total freedom. And he demanded only total commitment. As those who stood before him accepted the promise and the demand, they found themselves on the launching pad for the most exciting journey of spiritual transformation there has ever been.

It is the same Jesus, with the same message, who is changing lives and renewing communities throughout the world today. We may not be marginalized either physically or economically, but the person has not been born who is not in some deep way wounded and hurting. Those who appear externally to be the most self-sufficient are sometimes the most vulnerable.

A couple of years ago, I found myself sitting in a plane next to an obviously rich and successful businessman. Not quite next to him, for it was a row of three seats and between the two of us was an empty place. Its message was pretty clear: we were not meant to speak to each other. Nor did we for some considerable time. Not until the flight attendant arrived with a drink, and as a tray was passed along the row our eyes met for an instant. It was enough to break the ice, and we began a tentative conversation. As we talked, this man confided in me that he had problems. That very morning he had slammed the door of his home for the last time. His marriage was under stress. His growing children were giving cause for concern. And he was personally unfulfilled. The only thing to do was to leave them to get on with it, and try to find satisfaction alone somewhere else.

I was actually on my way to a religious conference where I was scheduled to give an address on the relevance of the Christian gospel to the modern world. I knew that I could not deliver that address with integrity if I did not share my faith in Christ with this person. But how? Frankly, I had no idea. So I did what most of us do when we are in a real fix: I prayed. A silent, momentary prayer that God would give me the words to say. Before I had time to think about it I found myself asking a question. 'Do you know God?' I said to the person alongside me. At that very instant my whole life seemed to flash before my eyes — like the last moments of a drowning man. What a stupid thing to say, I thought. Why had I not said something more conventional? Like, 'Have you been to church lately?' Or, 'Have you thought of consulting a priest?' Even, perhaps, 'Have you read the Bible?' Or whatever. But that was just wishful thinking. I had already asked my question.

If the question surprised me, the answer stunned me completely. 'As a matter of fact, I don't,' my companion replied, 'but if you know something about God, I'd like to know more.' So we spent the rest of the journey talking about some of the same subjects we have looked at in this book. At the end of the flight, we went our separate ways.

Then two or three weeks later I had a letter from this same person. In it, he told me how at his destination he could not stop thinking about our conversation. He had gone into a church that happened to be standing open, and there he prayed as best he knew how that, if God was for real, he would somehow intervene directly in his life. In due course, his business was completed and he had to face going home again. For all his bravado, he had nowhere else to stay. In any case, that would be a real test for God. When he finally returned, he was surprised to receive a warm welcome from his wife. Even more surprised to hear what she had to say.

The morning he left home, she too had felt it was all over. As she left her children at the school gate, she shared her feelings with another mother. A mother who was planning to go to a neighbourhood Bible study group that very day. The two of them went together. She was immediately attracted by the message of Jesus, and the warmth of the group. In fact, the group prayed for the husband on the plane — at exactly the moment that I was in conversation with him. As a direct result, it seemed, both husband and wife had met God in a new and challenging way that has subsequently transformed their marriage, their family, and their entire outlook on life. For my part, I was surprised to discover that my companion was not only a successful businessman: he was the chief executive of the airline. And the seat between us was empty because he had booked it to make sure no one spoke to him!

That man is typical of thousands of good and honest souls in today's world. Outwardly prosperous, inwardly bankrupt — hurting and wounded, yet not knowing where to turn for personal healing. To people like that, the message of Jesus is simple. 'Come to me,' he says in Matthew chapter 11, 'all of you who are tired from carrying heavy loads, and I will give you rest.'

For those who are honestly searching for spiritual meaning, personal transformation, inner healing, and harmony with the world and its people, his call is as irresistible today as it was then. And — as millions will happily affirm — his power to change things through the work of the Holy Spirit is undiminished. The Bible does not offer an escape route from the harsh realities of everyday life. It does not encourage us to think that God can be found by distancing ourselves from other people and the concerns of this world. On the contrary, it offers hope where we are. This is God's world. He loves it and all who live in it. He has shared it with us through the person of Jesus Christ. He can transform even the darkest corner with the brilliance of his own personal presence, and equip us with the power of his Spirit to do his will. For all genuine searchers after truth, that has got to be good news. The best news of all.

A selection of top titles from LION PUBLISHING

COPING WITH DEPRESSION	Myra Chave-Jones	£1.50	☐
HELL'S ANGEL	Brian Greenaway	£2.25	☐
IRINA	Dick Rodgers	£2.50	☐
ON THE SIDE OF THE ANGELS	John Smith	£2.99	☐
SINGLE PARENT	Maggie Durran	£1.95	☐
THE WAY OF JESUS	Bruce Farnham	£2.25	☐
BELIEF IN A MIXED SOCIETY	Christopher Lamb	£3.95	☐
CHRISTIANITY ON TRIAL	Colin Chapman	£4.95	☐
C. S. LEWIS	William Griffin	£5.95	☐
FACE TO FACE WITH CANCER	Marion Stroud	£3.95	☐
ISLAM AND CHRISTIANITY	Georges Moucarry	£4.95	☐
THE STRESS MYTH	Richard Ecker	£3.95	☐
MAKING UNEMPLOYMENT WORK	Michael Moynagh	£3.95	☐
WHOSE PROMISED LAND?	Colin Chapman	£3.50	☐

All Lion paperbacks are available from your local bookshop or
newsagent, or can be ordered direct from the address below. Just tick the
titles you want and fill in the form.

Name (Block letters) ....

Address ....

....

Write to Lion Publishing, Cash Sales Department, PO Box 11,
Falmouth, Cornwall TR10 9EN, England.

Please enclose a cheque or postal order to the value of the cover price
plus:

UK: 60p for the first book, 25p for the second book and 15p for each
additional book ordered to a maximum charge of £1.90.

OVERSEAS: £1.25 for the first book, 75p for the second book plus 28p
per copy for each additional book.

BFPO: 60p for the first book, 25p for the second book plus 15p per copy
for the next seven books, thereafter 9p per book.

Lion Publishing reserves the right to show on covers and charge new
retail prices which may differ from those previously advertised in the text
or elsewhere, and to increase postal rates in accordance with the Post
Office.